I0006827

Is Your Computer Bugged?

Protecting Your Computer From Cyber Attack

Also by Glenn G. Jacobs
with co-author C. A. Lindsay

The Samson Process

Is Your Computer Bugged?

Protecting Your Computer From Cyber Attack

~~~~~~~~~~~~~~~~~~~~~~~

Glenn G. Jacobs

 Cyber Cop Series

Copyright ©2011 by Glenn G. Jacobs
Art Copyright ©2010, 2011 by Geisel Artists and C.A. Lindsay

All rights reserved. No part of this book may be reproduced in any form, except for the quotation of brief passages in reviews, without prior permission from:

Creative Commerce LLC
P.O. Box 131242
Carlsbad CA 92013

www.bookartcorner.com

First Edition: March 2011

Jacobs, Glenn G.
   Is Your Computer Bugged? Protecting Your Computer from Cyber Attack
   ISBN: 978-1-4357-9752-9

DISCLAIMER: All information contained in this book represents the best available to us in the rapidly changing field of Cyber Security. All information is presented "as-is" without warranty. All risks associated with any configurations or configuration changes suggested in this book are assumed totally by the User. The author and the publisher shall have no liability to any person or entity with respect to the information contained within this book.

No network penetration of any kind occurred during the development of this book.

NETGEAR™ is a trademark of NETGEAR, Inc. Windows® is a registered trademark of Microsoft Corporation. Linux is a registered trademark of Linus Torvalds. (Linux®). Apple Computer , Mac, and Mac OS X® are trademarks of Apple, Inc. Other brand and product names referenced herein are trademarks or registered trademarks of their respective holders.

Printed in the United States of America
Lulu Books
North Carolina USA

For my Internet User community

whom I strive to protect from cyber attack

Acknowledgements

Special thanks to the Geisel Family artists for their talented contributions of bug art.

I must also thank C.A. Lindsay, without whose artistic contributions and constant encouragement this book would not be possible.

Additional special thanks goes to Ms. Ola, whose supportive descriptions and forwarding of the email attack against her certainly will help protect others.

I would also like to acknowledge the San Diego chapters of the Information Systems Security Association (ISSA), High Technology Crime Investigation Association (HTCIA), Securing Our eCity, The Security Network (TSN), and other cyber security groups that raised my awareness to the constant cyber security threat.

CONTENTS

Introduction

About The Author

INTRODUCTION

Imagine sitting in a room inside a gigantic library where you can access the knowledge of the entire planet from a convenient desktop. In this library, you can instantly view worldwide news events in "real-time" as they happen, communicate instantly with family and friends, pursue any number of academic venues, and conduct and promote your business.

You may have already guessed that this universal "library" I am referring to already exists – as today's World Wide Web, also known as the Internet. Indeed, the Internet supplies the incredible demand we all have today for instant information, communication, entertainment, gaming, social contact, and business transactions. What was science-fiction a few decades ago is now a convenience we take for granted.

Unfortunately, criminals, hackers, and other undesirable elements have discovered that they can use the inherent security flaws of the Internet to invade your private Web surfing experience. They can steal personal information, business communications, and even money from your bank account.

As shown by the illustrations in this book, intrusions by hackers can result in the theft of passwords and sensitive data, as well as the manipulation and crippling of computer functions.

It is thus my hope that this book will help the reader avoid the potential loss of personal data and financial freedom resulting from a cyber attack.

I chose *not* to describe in this book how personal computers work – how the various components such as processor units and memory chips interact with hard drives and myriad software packages to provide the User (you) with a precision computing experience.

However, throughout this book there *will* be many references to computer system network elements. These include those magnificent routers that hand-off the data from the World Wide Web to your PC, and the protective firewalls that hold off the invading hordes of hostile data packets, but the information will be limited to the specific functions and security risks being discussed.

Please note that the recommendations and configuration concepts described in this book apply equally to PCs using the Microsoft Windows®, Apple Computer Mac OS X®, and Linux® families of operating systems. However, configuration screen displays and functions will vary with different operating systems, router manufacturers, and email and Internet browser software.

Please also note that *all operating systems (Mac OS X, Microsoft Windows, and Linux) are constantly under attack by cyber criminals.*

When you see the "BUG" symbol throughout this book, it is referring to a serious **security risk** described in the nearby text on that page. This risk involves a bad computer network configuration decision or other security risk.

The author affirms that it is illegal to penetrate any computer network or retrieve private data without the written explicit consent of the network owner. Federal laws impose fines and possible jail sentences for illegal network activity. DO NOT ILLEGALLY PENETRATE ANY COMPUTER NETWORK. STAY OUT OF JAIL!

Let's get started! After constantly being informed how Wireless Internet computer networks ("Wireless Fidelity", or "WiFi") are broken into by hackers on a daily basis, I chose to begin in Chapter 1 by presenting how to minimize the threats resulting from this convenient, ever-present, and frequently insecure method of Internet access.

Let us begin, then, by seeing how Wireless Internet is a security risk, and what steps can be taken to reduce the risk.

Chapter 1

Wireless Internet is a Security Risk!

Welcome to the wireless 'Net !
A security risk that you can bet
Hackers will surely try to pry
Into your PC so they can spy
And reach personal data they often get.

Glenn G. Jacobs, geek poet

What is Wireless Fidelity (WiFi)?

Wireless Internet ("Wireless Fidelity" or "**WiFi**") is a popular system for granting wireless Internet access to laptop and other PCs using radio waves for distances of up to 300-800 feet. Once limited primarily to coffeshops (risky) and airports (even more risky), WiFi systems are now used in a great number of people's homes and businesses **because of the convenience and cost reduction resulting from not having to run Internet cables all through the building.**

 ### WiFi Usage Personal and Financial Risks

Personal Data Loss is the most obvious risk associated with **unprotected** (improperly configured) WiFi networks. If your WiFi network is not protected, your personal data may even be compromised accidentally by well-intentioned entities. One example is that of a prominent search engine corporation inadvertently "harvesting" personal data from unprotected WiFi networks during what should have been routine Internet geographical mapping activity:

"…. [a famous Search Engine Corporation] broke…privacy laws [in Massachusetts, Canada, and Italy] when it accidentally collected personal information from **unsecured wireless networks**…. An investigation…found complete emails, addresses, usernames and passwords. Even a list…of people suffering from certain medical conditions was collected."

San Jose Mercury News 10/20/2010

If you use an unprotected WiFi network the following may happen:

- Your email and "chat" messages may be intercepted
- Your usernames and passwords for financial and other websites may be intercepted
- Your website transactions may also be intercepted, ie, financial / medical and others

Financial Loss often follows the loss of personal data. The theft of credit card, banking, and investment accounts is the primary goal of almost all cyber criminals.

 ### WiFi Usage Potential Legal Risks

You may also be placed at risk or held liable for the following unauthorized use of *your* **unprotected** (improperly configured) WiFi network:

- "Simple" Internet "Web surfing" of harmless content by neighbors. This is because Internet cable and DSL (phone line) providers can prosecute you in several states for "allowing your paid Internet service to be used by others."
- Illegal downloads of "pirated" copyrighted music and/or movies.

- Download of illicit video/picture content

"....A feud between neighbors has left one man facing prison after he hacked his neighbor's WiFi connection and sent a threatening e-mail to the U.S. Vice President...."

eWeek.com 12/22/2010

I frequently hear people joking about how their own home wireless Internet systems are frequently used by their neighbors to get "Free WiFi" service. They may lose their humorous outlook if law enforcement agents come knocking on their door investigating downloads of illegal material.

Typical WiFi Home/Business Network

WiFi home system setup is (deceptively) simple. The User (you) requests or does the following:

- A small "modem" device is plugged into the Internet/TV cable (or into a high-speed telephone line such as "DSL") to provide your home or business a connection to the World Wide Web. This modem is usually supplied by your cable TV (or DSL telephone service) provider.

- A small, usually separate, "Wireless Router" (combination "digital traffic filter" / radio transmitter), is plugged into the modem so it can accept only *your* digital traffic packets. The Wireless Router then transmits Internet data throughout your home or business location using its antennae. The Wireless Router is sometimes purchased separately by the home or business User after a decision to "go wireless". In other cases, the modem/router functions may be combined into one block of hardware supplied by your cable TV (or DSL telephone service) provider.

  A Router's function, whether Wireless or Wired-only, is to restrict the delivery of Internet digital data to that addressed to the computer (s) within your home or business network. A Router behaves very much like a **gatekeeper** at an exclusive community, allowing delivery packages to enter the neighborhood only if they are addressed to one of its residents.

This chapter will focus on keeping intruders out of your *Wireless* Internet system, while **Chapter 2** will present security protections that apply to *both* Wired-only and Wireless Routers.

A typical WiFi Internet System is shown in **Figure 1-1**.

Figure 1-1. Typical Home WiFi System

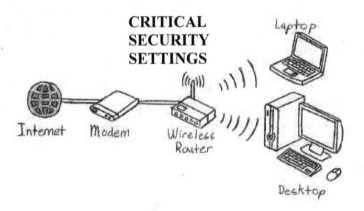

WiFi Router Hardware – Older "G" Series

1. The older *Institute of Electrical and Electronic Engineers* (IEEE) 802.11 *"G"* standard (circa 2003) WiFi Wireless Routers operate at a frequency of 2.4 GHz. This is in the same "neighborhood" as microwave ovens and some cordless phones and baby monitors.

2. These once popular *"G"* Routers are rapidly disappearing from retail store shelves in favor of faster Router hardware.
3. WiFi Users in the USA choose from one of 11 channels. To avoid interference, Users experiment with changing their WiFi channels between 1, 6, and 11 until local interference stops.
4. Data transfer is up to 54 MB/s, making a *"G"* Router suitable for home and small business locations such as coffee shops. A hacker's nearby WiFi network intrusion may obviously slow your home network's performance.
5. Typical radio range of 300 feet - **a hacker's playground.** It is often difficult to spot a WiFi intruder due to their physical distance from your home/business.
6. Most *"G"* Routers compatible with the even older "A" and "B" systems.
7. *"G"* Routers automatically change data rates to accommodate for workload.

WiFi Router Hardware –Newest "N" Series

1. The newer *Institute of Electrical and Electronic Engineers* (IEEE) 802.11 *"N"* standard (circa 2009) WiFi Wireless Routers operate at 2 frequency bands - 2.4 GHz and the older 5 GHz band, enabling the Router to "frequency hop" and avoid some forms of interference. This is in the same "neighborhood" as microwave ovens and some cordless phones and baby monitors.
2. The popular *"N"* Routers now dominate retail store shelves since they are faster and offer longer physical range.
3. Most new laptops incorporate *"N"*-standard Wireless Network Interface Cards (NICs). Wireless NICS are radio transceivers.
4. WiFi Users in the USA still choose from one of 11 channels. To avoid interference, Users typically will experiment with changing their WiFi channels between 1, 6, and 11 until local interference stops.
5. **GREATER SPEED!** Data transfer is up to 300 MB/s, making a *"N"* Router more than sufficient for home and small business locations such as coffee shops. A hacker's nearby WiFi network intrusion is unlikely to attract attention by slowing your home network's performance.

6. **GREATER DISTANCE!** Typical radio range is up to 800 feet or more - **a hacker's paradise!** It is now typically impossible to spot a WiFi intruder because of their physical distance from your home/business.
7. Most *"N"* Routers are compatible with the older "G" systems.
8. *"N"* Routers automatically accommodate for workload.
9. Some *"N"* Routers use MIMO (Multiple Input, Multiple Output) technology for utilizing up to 3 or 4 antennas for wireless communications to increase range. *"N"* hardware transmits several WiFi streams in different directions to achieve faster connectivity. Interference problems may worsen.

Configuring Your WiFi Router to Minimize Security Risks

1. **GETTING STARTED:** **Find Router's Internal IP Address, Default Username, and Default Password**

Verify your WiFi Router's Internal Admin website IP address, default username, and default password. These are listed within your Router's manufacturer's installation or user's manual.

If you do not have your Router's default username/password/IP address, do the following:

a. **Obtain your Wireless Router's model number.** The Model Number is displayed on the Router casing itself. It is visible on the front panel, rear panel, or the bottom label. (For this chapter we have chosen a popular WiFi Router, the **Netgear WNR3500L**).

b. After determining your Wireless Router's model number, refer to **Appendix A**, *"Default Router Settings, Related Web Links, and Last Resort Password Reset"*. **Appendix A** provides instructions regarding finding your Router's

Internal IP Address, default username, and default password.

In **Appendix A,** there is, of course, a reference to the popular **Netgear WNR3500L** WiFi Router, as shown in Figure **1-2.**

Figure 1-2. Netgear WNR3500L Router Default Settings

ROUTER MANUFACTURER	MODEL	IP ADDRESS	DEFAULT ADMIN USERNAME	DEFAULT ADMIN PASSWORD
Netgear	WNR3500L	192.168.1.1 or www. routerlogin.net	admin	password

Write the factory default Router "Admin" *password* down. We will change it shortly (ABSOLUTELY ESSENTIAL).

NOTE: PROPER SECURITY SETTINGS DURING WIRELESS ROUTER SOFTWARE SETUP ARE EXTREMELY CRITICAL.

IMPROPER ROUTER SOFTWARE SETTINGS MAY ALLOW HACKERS AND OTHER HOSTILE ENTITIES TO EASILY BREAK INTO YOUR SYSTEM AND STEAL PASSWORDS AND OTHER IMPORTANT DATA !

c. If you need further help obtaining your WiFi Router's Internal Admin website **IP address**, in **Appendix B** I have described the procedure for obtaining the Router IP address by using your hardwired PC to directly request the information and display it onscreen.

2. NEXT STEP: Make Sure the Lights are On

Verify that your modem is plugged into your Internet/TV cable (or into a high-speed telephone line such as "DSL") to provide your home or business a connection to the World Wide Web. **Verify that your modem is "on" as indicated by its display lamps**. Most modems have a dedicated lamp labeled "Internet", indicating that the modem is connected to the World Wide Web.

Verify that your modem is connected by its own Ethernet network cable to your Wireless Router. Make sure that your Wireless Router is "on." Most Routers also have dedicated "Power On" lamps **that glow green**. Many also have lamps labeled "WAN" ("Wide Area Network") or "Internet," indicating that the Router is ready to receive packets of World Wide Web data from the modem.

NOTE: With some modem vendors I have observed that the modem power must be switched off and then back on (so-called "power cycling") so that it can properly detect the Router.

3. Connect Your WiFi Router to Your PC Cable

During any Router setup or system maintenance activity (including this chapter's security settings upgrades), the WiFi Router **(Figure 1-3) must be connected to your PC with an Ethernet network cable (Figure 1-4)**. This permits the User to change the Wireless Router passwords and settings while avoiding being "locked out" of the Router "Administration" screens. The Ethernet network cable connection is also required before switching the "Wireless" function on and off, if needed.

Figure 1-3. WiFi Router with Available Ethernet Cable Sockets to Connect to Your PC

Figure 1-4. Ethernet Cable Used to Connect WiFi Router to Your PC for "Administration"

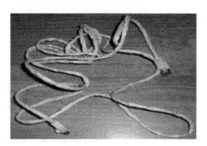

Verify that a PC is connected by an Ethernet network cable to one of the available Wireless Router Ethernet sockets shown in **Figure 1-3**.

4. Log in to Router IP Address Using Your Browser

With your PC booted up and ready for work, type your WiFi Router's IP Address (**192.168.1.1** for this chapter's Netgear example) into the top address bar of your Internet Browser, such as Firefox, as shown in **Figure 1-5.**

Figure 1-5. WiFi Router Admin Login Screen

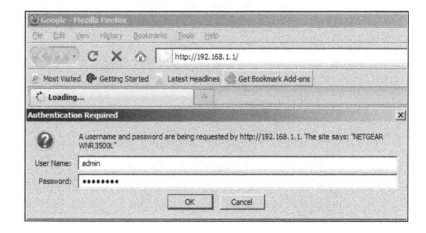

The "Authentication Required" dialog box will appear. Note the **admin** User Name.

Type in your WiFi Router's default password (such as **password** for Netgear) and click on **OK**.

5. Initially "Turn Off" WiFi Radio Transmitter

Turn off the Wireless Router "Radio" Transmitter until we can strengthen the WiFi security.

 This will present eavesdroppers from observing our security changes. This is done by **un**-checking the "**Enable Wireless Router Radio**" checkbox as shown in **Figure 1-6**.

Figure 1-6. Disable Router's "Wireless Radio"

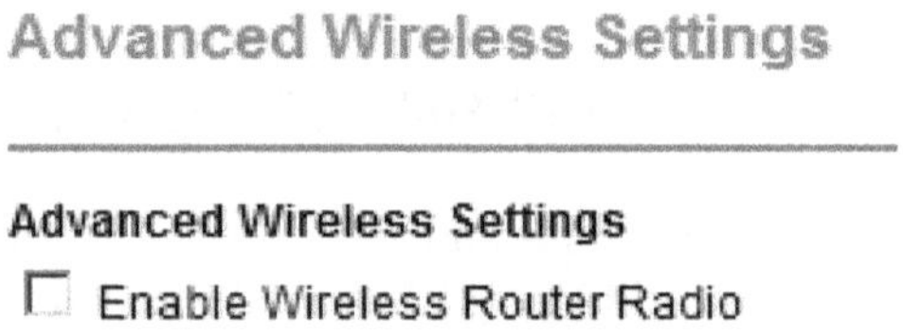

Advanced Wireless Settings

Advanced Wireless Settings
☐ Enable Wireless Router Radio

Then click "**Apply**"

After switching the Wireless transmitter off, you will still communicate with the WiFi Router's internal Admin website *though the network cable* running between your PC and your WiFi Router.

6. OPTIONAL: "Turn Off" WiFi Username ("SSID") Broadcast

If your intended WiFi User community (typically laptop Users) is running newer PC operating systems such as Microsoft Windows 7 or Linux, they will **not** need your WiFi Username to be "broadcasted." I then suggest you disable the WiFi Username ("SSID") Broadcast by **un-**checking the "Enable SSID Broadcast" checkbox as shown in **Figure 1-7**.

Figure 1-7.   OPTIONAL: Disable WiFi Username ("SSID") Radio Broadcast

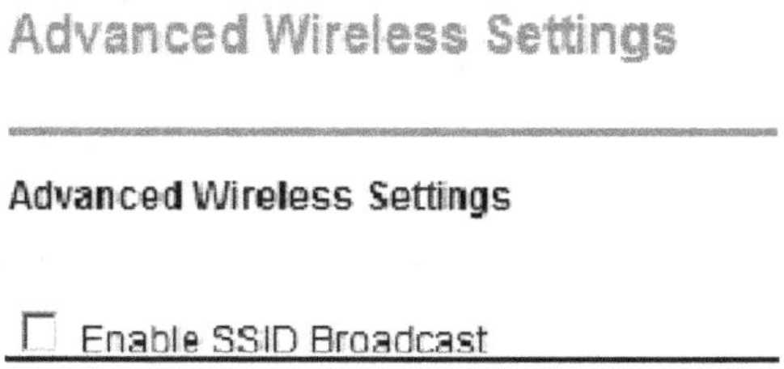

Advanced Wireless Settings

Advanced Wireless Settings

☐ Enable SSID Broadcast

Then click "**Apply**"

This OPTIONAL step will **prevent** your WiFi Router from unnecessarily displaying your WiFi Login Username (SSID) over the airwaves in your neighborhood, which is seen inside everyone's laptop's list of easy-to-use public "Login" screens.

 Hackers and other hostile entities use these Router-broadcasted lists of WiFi Login screens when they drive through neighborhoods as part of efforts to break into other people's networks.

However, I have observed some cases where the WiFi Username (SSID) broadcast *is* necessary. One example is when the intended WiFi User community (typically laptop Users) is **running older operating systems**. In this rare situation it is suggested that you leave the "Enable SSID Broadcast" checkbox **checked** (enabled).

7.   Change Your WiFi Login Username (SSID)

Change the WiFi Login Username (SSID) to an obscure mixture of *at least 10 letters and numbers* that will **NOT INDICATE YOUR PERSONAL OR BUSINESS NAME, YOUR HOME OR BUSINESS BUILDING LOCATION, OR THE NAME OF YOUR ROUTER'S MANUFACTURER!**

 Many home or business WiFi networks operate with the WiFi Login Username (SSID) still set to the manufacturer's factory default setting – **the name of the Router manufacturer!** This bad configuration practice broadcasts valuable information to a potential WiFi hacker.

 Many home WiFi networks operate with the WiFi Login Username (SSID) set to the **owner's street location or personal name**! This bad configuration practice provides valuable information to potential burglars, muggers, voyeurs, stalkers, and other undesirables.

An **example** of a recommended WiFi Login Username (SSID) is shown in **Figure 1-8.**

Figure 1-8. Use Obscure WiFi Login Username (SSID)

Wireless Settings

Wireless Network
Name (SSID):

g28hymupx

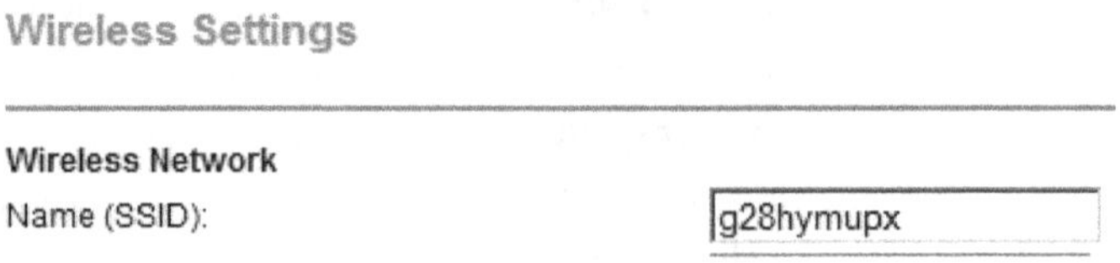

Then click "**Apply**"

Write your new WiFi Login Username (SSID) down and keep it in a safe place. Your SSID is the "User Name" required for you and all legitimate wireless Users to connect their laptop PCs to the Internet using your WiFi system. This is half of the login process. The other half is the WiFi User password, commonly called the "Passphrase" or "Personal Shared Key."

8. Set Your WiFi Encryption "Security Option" to WPA-2 With Strong "Passphrase"

Encryption (ABSOLUTELY ESSENTIAL) converts your WiFi radio transmissions into a form unintelligible to hackers and other hostile entities.

Some home or business Users leave their WiFi systems **un**encrypted (or weakly encrypted), often leading to disastrous security breaches.

Use the WiFi Router Security Option settings shown in **Fig 1-9**.

Figure 1-9. WiFi Security Option Settings: WPA-2 PSK / AES

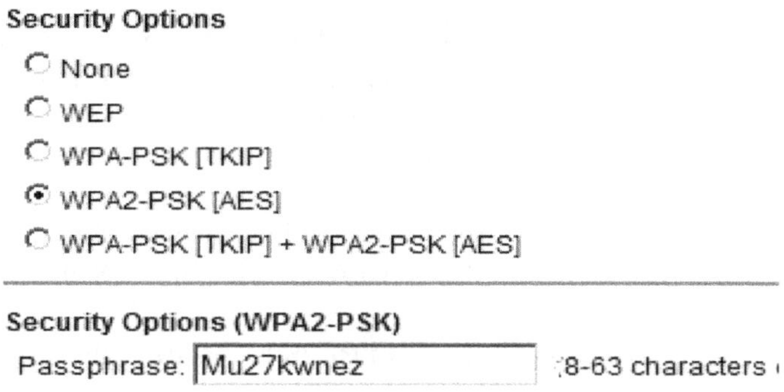

Security Options

- ○ None
- ○ WEP
- ○ WPA-PSK [TKIP]
- ⊙ WPA2-PSK [AES]
- ○ WPA-PSK [TKIP] + WPA2-PSK [AES]

Security Options (WPA2-PSK)

Passphrase: Mu27kwnez   ;8-63 characters ‹

Then click "**Apply**"

Note the comments below on the suggested WiFi Router security settings:

a. *Use Security Option* **WPA2-PSK** ("WiFi Protected Access version **2**, **Pre-Shared Key**"): This is the best **Security Option** for home and small business systems as of this writing.

b. *Use "Strong" Encryption:* **AES** ("Advanced Encryption Standard"). This is the best **encryption** standard currently available for WiFi. **AES** meets requirements for U.S. Government data.

c. *Use "Strong" Passphrases:* A **Passphrase** is your WiFi Login Password (also known as the "**Pre-Shared Key**," or "**PSK**") that you and your home/business Users will "**share**" to access your Wireless Internet network. Set your **Passphrase** to be an obscure mixture of *at least 10 letters and numbers* that will be impossible for hackers to guess. Do *not* use numbers in sequence (i.e. "12345" etc). Hackers can guess any number sequence!

9. Never User WEP or WPA (old version) Encryption

a. DO NOT USE Wired Equivalent Privacy (**WEP**) "protection." It can be broken in less than 1 minute, enabling hackers to steal sensitive data.

b. DO NOT USE the older **WPA /TKIP** (WiFi Protected Access) "protection". **WPA /TKIP** can be broken in less than 15 minutes, enabling hackers to steal sensitive data.

c. Use stronger protection such as **WPA2-PSK/AES** (WiFi Protected Access **2** with AES encryption).

10. Set Your WiFi Router "Admin" Password

Change your WiFi Router **Admin password** to an obscure mixture of letters and numbers at least 10 characters long that will be impossible for hackers to guess. Do not use numbers in sequence (i.e. "12345"

etc.).   Hackers will guess any number sequence!!
Write down and keep your new **Admin password** in a
safe place. I recommend that only *you* have the **Admin
password** because it grants *you* the power to configure
your network's security settings.

Setting the Router **Admin password** to a value
impossible for hackers to guess is HYPER-CRITICAL
for network security.

A suprisingly large number of Users leave
their Router **Admin password** at its intial,
factory-set value (often *"password"*), enabling
hackers to seize control of their WiFi networks and steal
sensitive data.

Most WiFi "Admin" passwords appear as asterisks or
similar characters as you enter the new password, as
shown in **Figure 1-10.**

Figure 1-10. Set Router "Admin" Password

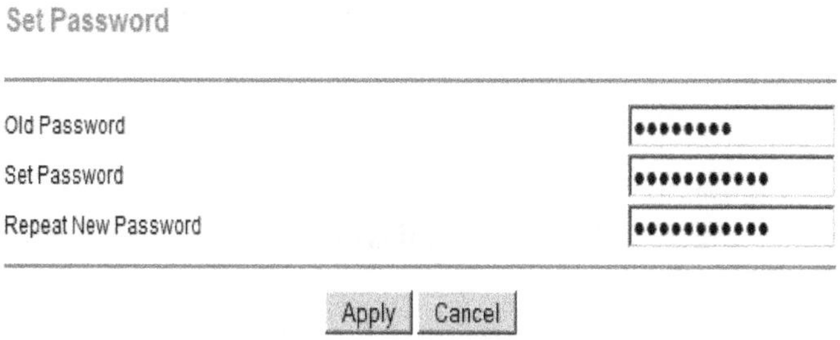

Set Password

Old Password	••••••••
Set Password	••••••••••••
Repeat New Password	••••••••••••

Apply   Cancel

Then click "**Apply**"

**11. Set WiFi Router Software Updates to
"Automatic"**

This will enable the Router vendor to download security and
other performance enhancements from the Internet to the
Router's internal microchip-embedded software (so-called
"firmware").   These downloads will then occur

whenever the "Admin" User (you) logs into the WiFi Router *internal* website (such as **192.168.1.1** for this chapter's Netgear Router example).

Click on the "Check for Updated Firmware Upon Log-in" checkbox as shown in **Figure 1-11**.

Figure 1-11. Set Router Software Updates to "Automatic"

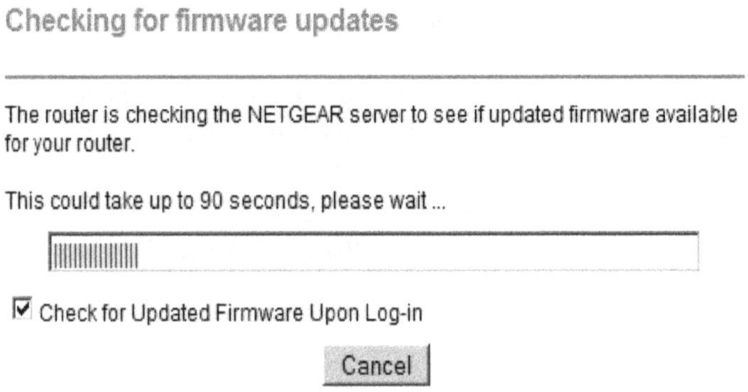

Checking for firmware updates

The router is checking the NETGEAR server to see if updated firmware available for your router.

This could take up to 90 seconds, please wait ...

☑ Check for Updated Firmware Upon Log-in

Cancel

12. Turn WiFi Radio Transmitter "Back On"

At this point we have strengthened the WiFi Router security.

We will now turn back on your Wireless Router's "Radio" Transmitter.

This is done by *checking* the "**Enable Wireless Router Radio**" checkbox as shown in **Figure 1-12**.

Figure 1-12. Enable Router's "Wireless Radio"

Advanced Wireless Settings

Advanced Wireless Settings
☑ Enable Wireless Router Radio

Then click "**Apply**"

13. OPTIONAL: Restrict WiFi Network Access to Specific Wireless Computers

One of the **OPTIONAL Admin** capabilities of Router software is to restrict Wireless access to *only* those PCs, usually laptops that you specifiy using a so-called "**Wireless Card Access List.**" Using this utility, the "Admin" User (you) enters several identifing parameters of each laptop's WiFi transmitter circuit ("Wireless Card") into a special list.

Each PC's WiFi Wireless transmitter card contains (and broadcasts) a special ID number ("*MAC Address*"). This ID number is used by the **Wireless Card Access List** option to provide access to the WiFi network to PCs you approve of.

The *advantage* of this **Wireless Card Access List** option is that it provides yet another obstacle to hackers and other hostile entities trying to break into your network.

The *disadvantage* of this option is that the Router "Admin" User (you) must log into the Router Admin internal website and **edit** the **Wireless Card Access List** *every time one of the below events occurs:*

- You wish to grant (or remove) WiFi network access to/from a *new* PC. This PC may be a laptop belonging to a family member, customer, client, or friend. You must then add or remove the special ID number (*"MAC Address"*) for each new PC that requires access to your network to or from the **Wireless Card Access List.**

- An existing PC (such as your laptop) undergoes a configuration change (such as a new WiFi Wireless Card being installed). You must then edit the **"Wireless Card Access List"** to include the new special ID number (*"MAC Address"*) of the PC in question.

If you do decide to utilize the WiFi Router "Admin" **Wireless Card Access List** option, do the following:

a. Use your "Admin" PC (usually a desktop) and click on the **"Set Up Access List"** button for the **"Wireless Card Access List"** utility, as shown in **Figure 1-12.**

Figure 1-12. Wireless Card Access List Utility

Advanced Wireless Settings

Wireless Card Access List	Set Up Access List

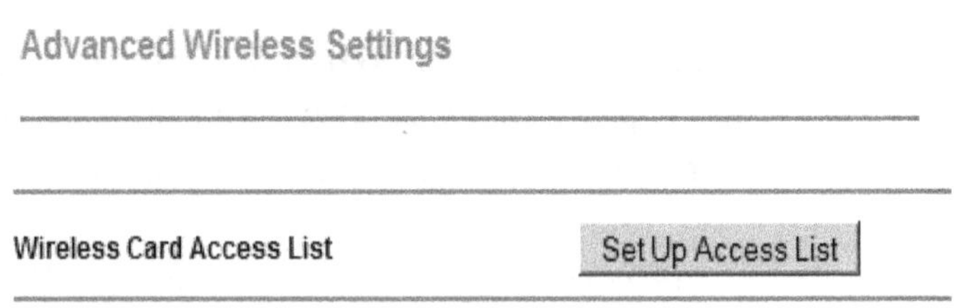

b. The **Wireless Card Access List** screen will be displayed. In our example the **Wireless Card Access List** is blank, as shown in **Figure 1-13.**

Figure 1-13. Wireless Card Access List Turned Off

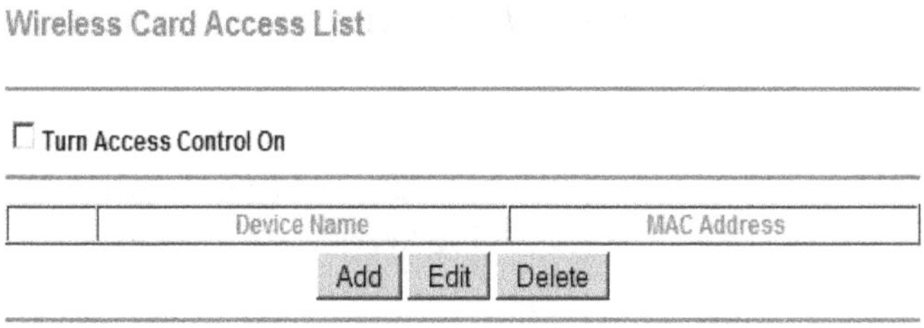

Wireless Card Access List
_____

☐ Turn Access Control On
_____

	Device Name	MAC Address
	Add	Edit	Delete	

_____

c. Verify that the **Turn Access Control On** checkbox is *un*checked for now, as as shown in **Figure 1-13.** This checkbox must always be unchecked before adding a new laptop to the **Wireless Card Access List.**

d. Turn on the laptop you wish to add to your Wireless Router's **Wireless Card Access List.**

Make sure your laptop's WiFi "Wireless Network Card" is on. With many laptops, the "**F2**" key switches the WiFi Network Card on and off.

Click on the Network icon located in the lower right corner of your laptop.Select your WiFi Network's **SSID** (wireless login username).

Log in with your laptop to your WiFi network using your recently assigned WiFi Login Username **(SSID)** and WiFi "**Passphrase**" (password).

e. Using your "Admin" PC, click on the **Add** button on the **Wireless Card Access List**.

Note that your *laptop* PC's IP Address, Device Name, and MAC (*Media Access Control/Network Interface Card*) Address are now automatically displayed in the **Available Wireless Cards** list, as shown in **Figure 1-13.**

Figure 1-13. Adding Laptop Wireless Card to Available Wireless Cards list

Wireless Card Access List

Available Wireless Cards

	Device Name	MAC Address
○	whitehat-laptop	00:22:43:a6:b0:1d

Wireless Card Entry

Device Name: [ ]

MAC Address: [ ]

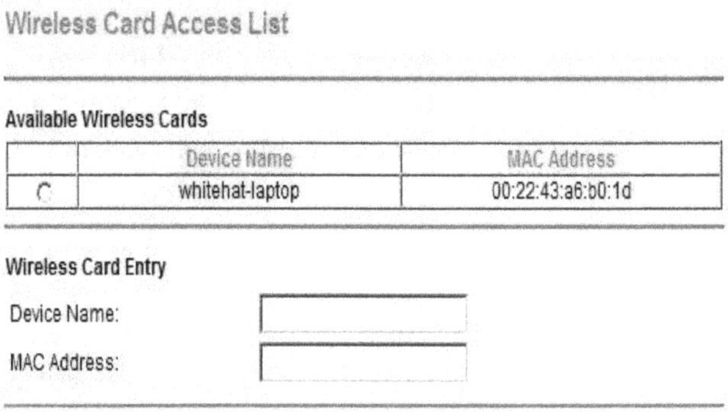

f. Click on the small "radio" option button to the left of the **Device Name,** as shown in Figure **1-14.**

Figure 1-14. Adding Laptop Wireless Card to Wireless Card Entry

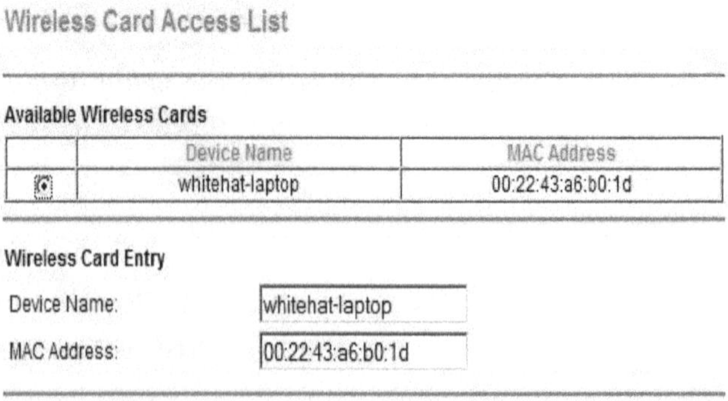

Wireless Card Access List

Available Wireless Cards

	Device Name	MAC Address
◉	whitehat-laptop	00:22:43:a6:b0:1d

Wireless Card Entry

Device Name: [whitehat-laptop]

MAC Address: [00:22:43:a6:b0:1d]

Note that your *laptop* PC's IP Address, Device Name, and MAC (*Media Access Control/Network Interface Card*) Address are now automatically displayed in the **Wireless Card Entry** list.

g. Verify that the **Turn Access Control On** checkbox is checked, as as shown in **Figure 1-15.** This checkbox must always be checked after adding a new laptop to the **Wireless Card Access List.**

Figure 1-15. Wireless Card Access List Turned On

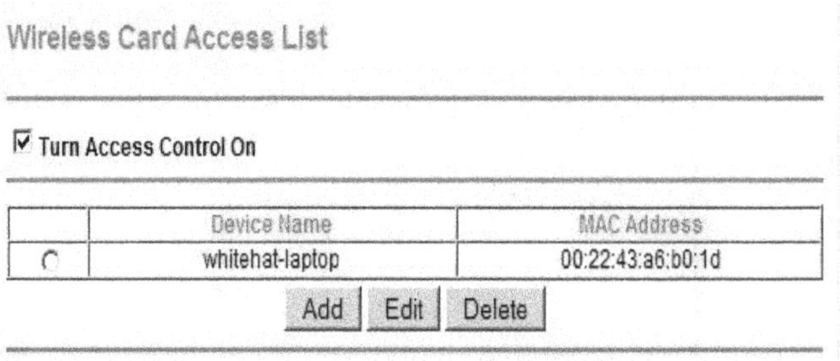

Wireless Card Access List

☑ Turn Access Control On

	Device Name	MAC Address
○	whitehat-laptop	00:22:43:a6:b0:1d

Add   Edit   Delete

Then click "**Apply**"

This completes my WiFi home/business network configuration security recommendations. Log out of the the WiFi Router "Admin" local website.

No discussion on WiFi security would be complete without a few cautionary real-life examples of *bad* WiFi configurations !

Examples of Multiple Bad WiFi Security Configurations

During a visit to a coffeeshop I switched on my laptop and clicked on the WiFi/Networking icon in the lower right-hand corner of the Microsoft Windows 7 screen. I then observed the multiple bad security configurations broadcasted **by the coffee shop and six other nearby WiFi networks!**

In order to protect their privacy, I disguised the names of the coffeeshop and all other networks I observed. In **Figure 1-16** we display the "*It's a Coffee*" coffeeshop's unsecured WiFi network status, as well as the other network names I disguised.

Figure 1-16. Bad WiFi Security Settings

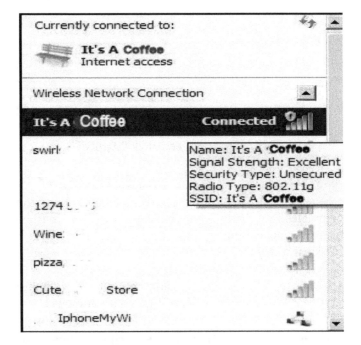

Let's now analyze each bad WiFi security setting shown in **Figure 1-16 .**

- The *"It's a Coffee"* Login Username (SSID) is broadcasted for all to see. This confirms the exact location of the coffeeshop as a target for computer hacking and possible physical intrusion.

- The *"It's a Coffee"* WiFi network is totally *"Unsecured"* (unencrypted), meaning that a hacker can use cyber attack software *to monitor all laptops connected to the coffeeshop WiFi network.* Hackers can then steal valuable information such as coffeeshop patrons' Web surfing habits, website passwords, and account numbers.

- The *"It's a Coffee"* WiFi network is broadcasting that it is using an older *"G"* series WiFi Router. The hacker can then use cyberattack software to probe for known weaknesses for the Router in question. The hacker will then penetrate the *"It's a Coffee"* networked accounting computers on the premises, and steal funds from the business.

- The remaning 4 nearby businesses (*"Swirl"* frozen dairy store, *"Wine"* liquor outlet, *"Pizza"* restaurant, and *"Cute clothing Store"*) all broadcast their WiFi Login Username (SSID) for everyone to see. This bad configuration decision identifies these businesses as hacker targets for the theft of both sales/ marketing intelligence *and* bank accounts.

- One nearby WiFi network broadcasted its owner's telephone number as the WiFi Login Username (SSID). This bad decision leaves the owner vulnerable to stalking activities by hostile entities.

• And, finally, one nearby WiFi network owner included in their WiFi Login Username (SSID) the expression "*iPhone MyWi.*" This bad decision informs a hacker that the owner's popular smartphone is connected to the WiFi network, making it vulnerable to attack and financial information theft. Smartphones are increasingly being used for online banking.

~~~~~~

What follows are a few of my recommendations for laptop WiFi network usage.

Laptop WiFi Usage Security Guidance:

1. About "Automatic Wireless Connections" (Automatic Login Once Your Laptop is Near a Wireless Network)

Most PCs, such, as those using MS Windows 7, permit the laptop User to save the WiFi connection username (SSID) and password (Passphrase) data for *any* desired network in a record called a "profile." The User may then set the given WiFi profile to "start connection automatically."

For your *Home* network this is acceptable. **Figure 1-17** shows the Manual WiFi connection setup required for a MS Windows 7 PC.

Figure 1-17. Manual WiFi Connection Setup on Laptop to Facilitate Automatic Connection

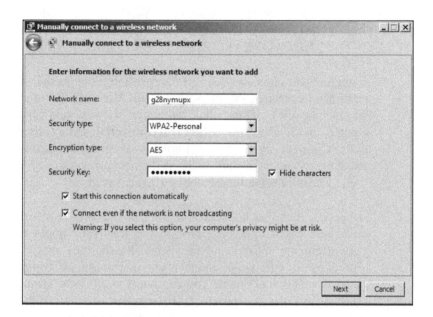

Note that **Figure 1-17** shows the following WiFi connection configuration decisions:

a. The "**Start the connection automatically**" checkbox is checked. This means when you are within radio range of your WiFi network (up to 300-800 feet) and your laptop's WiFi Network Interface Card (NIC) is switched "on," your laptop will automatically connect to the Internet.

b. The "**Connect even if the network is not broadcasting**" checkbox is checked. This means that your laptop will automatically connect through your WiFi network to the Internet even though, as I recommended in this chapter, that you not broadcast your WiFi username (SSID) over the airwaves.

This is OK for your Home network only – but *not* for the coffeeshop, the airport, or the business/industrial park.

 DO NOT PERMIT YOUR LAPTOP TO AUTOMATICALLY CONNECT TO ANY WIFI NETWORK OUTSIDE YOUR HOME.

I suggest you click on the WiFi/Networking icon in the lower right-hand corner of the PC screen (with Microsoft Windows 7 as our example). Then, click on "Open Network and Sharing Center" and *uncheck* the "**Start the connection automatically**" and "**Connect even if the network is not broadcasting**" checkboxes for each and every WiFi network *ouside of your home* whose information you have already saved.

I suggest that you connect *manually* to the WiFi network in your business workplace. This means that you should enter your username (SSID) and password (Passphrase) every time you need to wirelessly connect to your corporate computer network. This will enable you to review and briefly scrutinize (and verify) the "corporate WiFi network" to verify that it matches your company's stated requirements, such as encryption, to make sure your data is *not* being sent and received in "clear text" (readable to anyone within radio range).

 Hackers may attempt to trick you into "logging in" to their nearby illegal "rogue" WiFi network by broadcasting a username (SSID) *similar (or identical) to your legitimate corporate SSID.*

I also suggest that you *never* connect to airport, hotel, or coffeeshop WiFi networks for the following reasons:

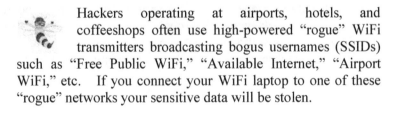 Hackers operating at airports, hotels, and coffeeshops often use high-powered "rogue" WiFi transmitters broadcasting bogus usernames (SSIDs) such as "Free Public WiFi," "Available Internet," "Airport WiFi," etc. If you connect your WiFi laptop to one of these "rogue" networks your sensitive data will be stolen.

Many legitimate public WiFi networks, such as those in coffeeshops, not only do not use encryption but openly broadcast this fact, along with their WiFi username (SSID). This was shown in the example in **Figure 1-16.** Hackers can then use any of numerous free tools such as *Firesheep* (released in 2010) to capture passwords and other sensitive data from laptops connected to unencrypted WiFi networks.

2. What about Wireless "Internet Connection Sharing"?

I suggest that you disable wireless "Internet Connection Sharing," including the Wireless Access Point ("**Virtual WiFi Miniport Adapter**") *built into Microsoft Windows 7.* This well-intentioned feature might enable hackers to connect to your PC (very bad) and to exploit your connection to the Internet (also very bad).

Locate the WiFi/Networking icon in the lower right-hand corner of the PC screen (with Microsoft Windows 7 as our example), as shown in **Figure 1-18.** As you move your cursor over the icon the expression "Internet access" will appear. Click on the icon.

Figure 1-18. MS Windows 7 Internet Access Icon

Then, click on the "Open Network and Sharing Center" link and disable the Microsoft **"Virtual WiFi Miniport Adapter."**

An alternative procedure, again using Microsoft Windows 7 as an example, would be to click on the "Start" menu button, then "Control Panel," then "System," then the "System Protection" menu link, then the "Hardware" tab.

Click on the "Device Manager" button shown in **Figure 1-18**.

Figure 1-18. "Device Manager" Button in MS Windows 7 System "Hardware" Tab

The "Device Manager" screen will then appear, as shown in **Figure 1-19.**

Right-click on the "Microsoft Virtual WiFi Miniport Adaper" link.

Figure 1-19. Right-Click on "Virtual WiFi Miniport Adapter" link

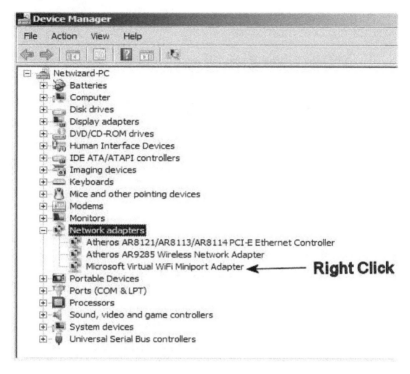

Click on the "*Disable*" choice that appears, as shown in **Figure 1-20.**

Figure 1-20. Disable WiFi Miniport

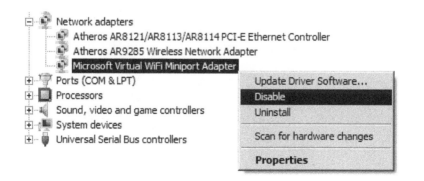

The "Disabling WiFi Miniport" confirmation box will appear, as shown in **Figure 1-21.**

Figure 1-21. Confirm Disabling WiFi Miniport

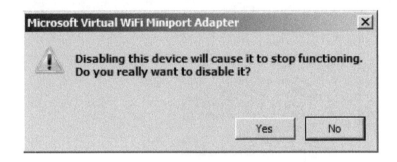

Click on the **"Yes"** button.

The "WiFi Miniport" will now be disabled. This will prevent hackers from connecting to your PC via WiFi and/or exploiting your connection to the Internet.

This completes my recommendations for making your home/business WiFi network more resistant to intrusion.

This first chapter has focused entirely on WiFi (Wireless Internet) security.   Let's now focus our attention on your computer system's first actual "solid" layer of protection from the hazards of the Internet.

This protective "flameproof" barrier, usually contained within the previously described **Router**, is aptly named the "**Firewall**".

Chapter 2

Routers and Firewalls – The Gatekeepers and Guardians

I forgot to switch my firewall on,
So all my computer portals were bare
For hackers and criminals inside to stare,
And now all my private data has gone
To locations I know not where

Glenn G. Jacobs, geek poet

What is a Firewall?

Let's return briefly to a description of the Internet – the marvelous, almost science-fiction collection of all of the world's knowledge – mentioned in this book's Introduction. Imagine you're sitting in our fantastic Internet "library" when suddenly you look up from your beautiful plasma screen and see an ocean of transparent glass window panes all around you. You can look out, and many others can look *in*.

In fact, there are 65,535 Internet "window panes" of two (or more) different data transmission types.

You are thus surrounded by **65,535 or more transparent portals** to the hostile outside world!

There suddenly doesn't seem to be much security provided by our magnificent Internet library, and doing *private* research or communication or business transactions doesn't seem very likely......

......unless you find a way to pull some shades down on the individual computer "ports" ("window panes") that you *don't* want. You must also simultaneously *inspect* what kind of data (and risk!) is being provided by the ports you *do* need to keep open.

This is exactly what a *firewall* does. It "pulls shades down on" (closes) ports that you don't need, and *inspects* data entering or leaving through the ports you must leave open for your particular Internet tasks, as shown in **Figure 2-1.**

**Figure 2-1. Firewall Protecting Your Network
By Restricting and Inspecting Data Ports**

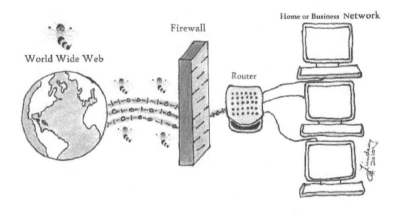

Note the "bug" symbols shown in the left section of **Figure 2-1**, showing serious potential **security threats** coming from the World Wide Web.

Let's consider an example of a data portal that is absolutely necessary: Port 80, used for delivering most *website* content to your PC. Unfortunately, Port 80 might also deliver hostile, destructive content in addition to legitimate data. The *inspection* function of the firewall *reduces* the probability of a portal being abused by a hostile entity.

I recommend that your home/business computer network utilize *2 SEPARATE TYPES OF FIREWALLS* to monitor and inspect incoming and outgoing data from and to the Internet. Each firewall offers separate security advantages to your network.

The Two Separate Firewalls – Router-based and PC-based

1. Router ("Hardware") Firewall

This firewall is referred to as a "hardware" firewall because its computer code is embedded in the memory microchips inside your Router. Hardware firewalls are *most* adept at stopping *incoming* Internet threats to all the PCs on their network. These incoming threats may include automated network scanning operations used in preparation for an attack against your system. Router hardware firewalls act as a first line of defense for your network.

2. PC-based ("Software") Firewall

Software firewalls are installed *on each individual PC's hard drive*. Installation is usually done via Internet download from the software vendor's web site, or from a purchased installation CD.

Software firewalls are usually automatically configured during installation. They permit certain other programs (such as email utilities and Internet browsers) to run on *each PC*.

Software firewalls are adept at stopping unauthorized *outgoing* communication to the Internet, and thus prevent transmission of your sensitive data to hostile parties.

In conjunction with *anti-virus* programs, software firewalls protect against downloaded viruses. Anti-virus programs will be discussed further in **Chapter 3**.

First, I'll present information about how to configure your Router's hardware firewall to resist intrusion.

Configuring Your Router ("Hardware") Firewall

1. Do Not Respond to "Pings" (Surveillance Test Signals) From the Internet (Unless Required by Corporate VPN)

"Pings" are Internet surveillance test signals sent to your computer's address ("IP Address") to see if your network is active. Their function is similar to someone knocking on the front door at your home address to see if you are there. If you respond by speaking or opening the door, the person can attack you.

At one time pings were exclusively used for legitimate network testing. It was then safe to allow them, just as it was once safe to open your front door when someone knocked on it.

Response to pings is sometimes required if you are required to connect to a corporate Virtual Private Network (VPN). NOTE: Depending upon the brand of Router you are using, the more formal term "**ICMP**" (Internet Control Message Protocol) may be displayed instead of the expression "ping."

Pings and ICMP are also, unfortunately, used by hackers not only to verify your network's exisence but, in large quantities, as virtual "bullets" to deliberately overload your system and make it crash (break down) during an automatically generated destructive flood of pings, aptly named a "Ping Flood."

In the example shown in **Figure 2-2** for our Netgear WNR3500NL Router, the "**Respond to Ping on Internet Port**" checkbox should be left *unchecked* unless pings are required by a corporate VPN.

Figure 2-2. Do Not Respond to Internet Pings

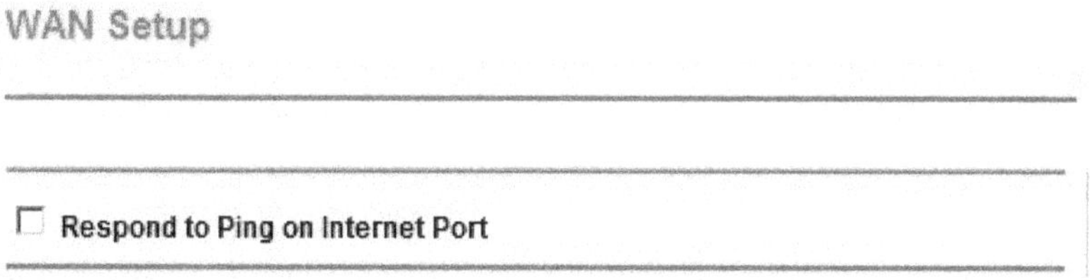

WAN Setup

☐ Respond to Ping on Internet Port

---

2. Block Port Scan Surveillance

"Port Scans" are Internet surveillance operations conducted against your computer to see which of its "ports" are open (accessible). This activity is similar to someone prowling around the windows at your home to see if any are open so that they may jump in and attack you.

Once the hacker has determined which computer port to "jump through" to access your network, they will attempt to do one or more of the following:

    a.   Extract sensitive information

    b. Overload your system with so many incoming data packets that it cannot service legitimate User requests for information. This kind of "overload assault" is called a "Denial of Service" (DoS) attack.

In the example shown in Figure 2-3 for our Netgear WNR3500NL Router, the "Disable Port Scan and Denial of Service (DoS) Protection" checkbox should be left *unchecked.*

Figure 2-3. Enable Protection against Port Scans and Denial of Service (DoS)

WAN Setup

☐ Disable Port Scan and DoS Protection

3. ALTERNATIVE CONFIGURATION EXAMPLE USED BY OTHER ROUTERS – Combined Selection Boxes for Blocking Internet Pings , Port Scans, and Denial of Service (DoS)

Alternatively, some Router Firewall internal Administration websites *combine into two User selection boxes* the choices for protection against Internet Pings, Port Scan, and Denial of Service (DoS), as shown in **Figure 2-4**.

In the example shown in **Figure 2-4,** the "**Block WAN** [Wide Area Network, or Internet] **Ping"** selection should be set to *Enabled* unless you are required to connect to a corporate Virtual Private Network (VPN).

In the example shown in **Figure 2-4,** the "**SPI** [Stateful Packet Inspection] **Mode"** selection should be set to *Enabled* **SPI** [Stateful Packet Inspection] examines the incoming packets to ensure that they are part of a "legitimate" connection to your network, and not part of a DoS attack or Port Scanning attack against your system.

Figure 2-4. Example of an Alternative User Screen For Router Security Setup:

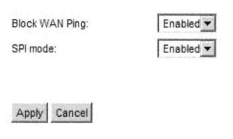

Then click **"Apply"**

4. **Block File Transfer Protocol ("FTP", Ports 20 and 21)**

File Transfer Protocol (FTP) has often in the past been used to transfer file data between PCs and personal websites or corporate file systems. FTP uses 2 ports: **Port 20** for the actual data transfer, and **Port 21** for command/control.

FTP transmits its login username/password as unencrypted "clear" text. **FTP is a security risk.** Computer viruses often are transmitted during FTP downloads from criminal as well as innocent (but infected) websites. Once installed on a PC, viruses often transmit *your* stolen personal and financial information to criminal websites via FTP.

Most websites and corporate networks now offer encrypted connections and special websites or networks ("Virtual Private Networks," or VPNs) as alternatives to FTP in order to minimize data transfer risk. An increasing number of corporations flat out do not permit their employees to utilize FTP, due to the security risk.

As shown in **Figure 2-5**, I suggest you access your Router's "Administrative" internal website and add FTP to the list of blocked services.

Figure 2-5.   Block File Transfer Protocol ("FTP")

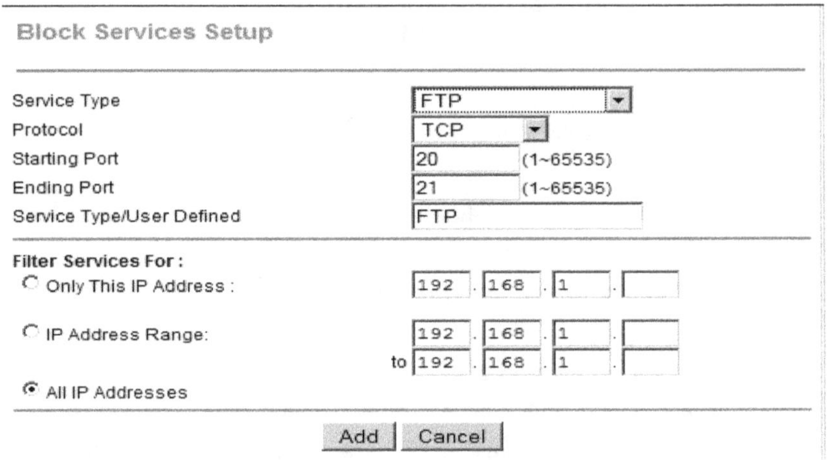

Block Services Setup

Service Type	FTP ▾
Protocol	TCP ▾
Starting Port	20 (1~65535)
Ending Port	21 (1~65535)
Service Type/User Defined	FTP

Filter Services For :

○ Only This IP Address :   192 . 168 . 1 .

○ IP Address Range: 192 . 168 . 1 .
          to 192 . 168 . 1 .

⊙ All IP Addresses

Add   Cancel

Then click "**Add**"

5.   Block Telnet and Internet Relay Chat (IRC)

I recommend that you repeat the above "Block Services" process and block **Telnet** and **Internet Relay Chat (IRC),** producing the result shown in Figure 2-6.

39

Figure 2-6. Block Telnet and IRC

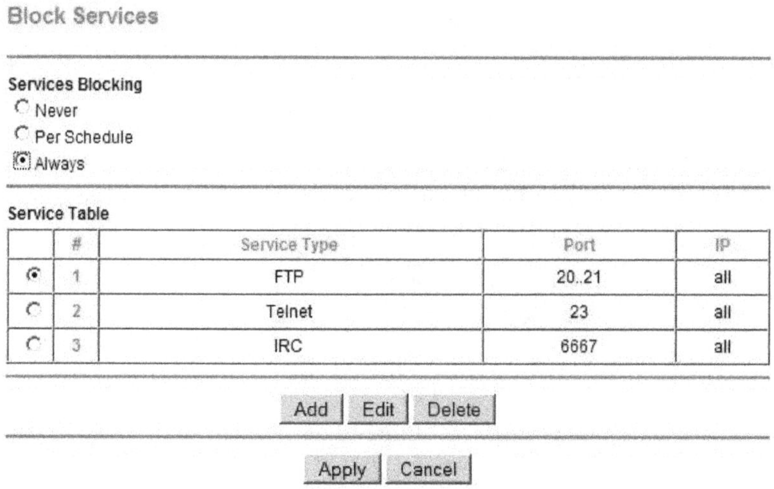

Block Services

Services Blocking
- ○ Never
- ○ Per Schedule
- ◉ Always

Service Table

	#	Service Type	Port	IP
◉	1	FTP	20..21	all
○	2	Telnet	23	all
○	3	IRC	6667	all

Add | Edit | Delete

Apply | Cancel

Then click **"Apply"**

Telnet has often in the past been used to communicate and transfer data between separate networks across the Internet. The User (you) launches client (PC-based) software, known as a "terminal emulator", and connects to the remote system. The PC software mimics the appearance and functionality of an early 1970s-era data terminal screen. **PCs use Port 23** for Telnet.

Telnet transmits its login password and data as unencrypted "clear" text. **Telnet is a security risk.** I recommend you block the Telnet service (Port 23), unless Telnet is specifically required for your home business.

Internet Relay Chat (IRC), as the name implies, enables free "chatroom" communications across the Internet. IRC became popular during the late-1980s and is still widely in use today. Although the majority of IRC networks (and their Users) are pefectly legitimate, the majority of IRC connections are *unencrypted*, leaving IRC networks susceptible to attack.

In addition, IRC is a primary mechanism for delivering Trojan viruses that turn your PC into a sleeping "bot," waiting to attack a specified network after receiving a "remote command." I will discuss this further in **Chapter 3**. Many corporations block IRC from their networks because of the security risk. I recommend you block the IRC service (**Port 6667**), unless IRC is specifically required for your home business.

This completes my recommendations for configuring your Router ("**Hardware**") firewall to improve network security. Next, I will present how to configure your PC-based ("**Software**") firewall to resist both incoming intrusion and unauthorized outgoing transmission of sensitive data.

Configuring Your PC Firewall to Improve Network Security

1. **GETTING STARTED:** Verify if any Previously installed Software Firewalls are present on your PC

NOTE: *Never **run** two or more **software (PC-based)** firewalls at the same time*. These will conflict with each other, similar to 2 doormen at a restaurant or bar entranceway stepping on each other's feet.

As part of my "cleanup" procedures, I frequently am required to remove multiple vendors' versions of **software firewalls** from my clients' PCs in order to stop or prevent these conflicts.

To view which software firewall programs are installed and running, I will use a Microsoft Windows 7 example. Click on the "Start" menu button, then "Control Panel," then the "Action Center."

As shown in **Figure 2-5**, click on the Security tab down arrow:

Figure 2-5. Click on Security tab down arrow

As shown in **Figure 2-6**, the "View installed firewall programs" link will appear. Click on this link.

Figure 2-6. Click on "View installed firewall programs"

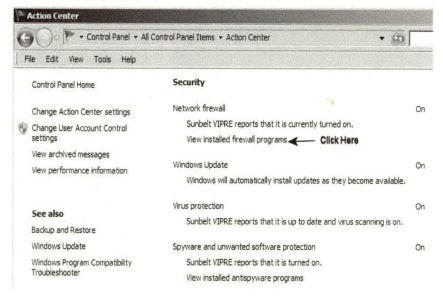

The list of installed software firewall programs will be displayed, along with their **Status** (Off/On). In our example, two software firewalls have been installed, but, (as required), only one software firewall (Sunbelt VIPRE) is "On" (running), as shown in **Figure 2-7**.

Figure 2-7. List of Installed Software Firewall Programs and their On/Off Status

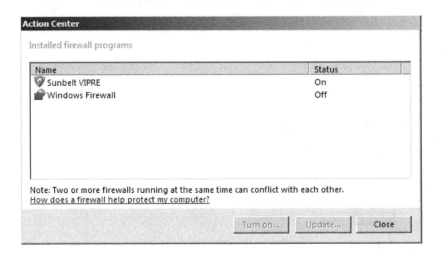

If more than one software firewall is shown as "On"(running), **click on the link to the undesired firewall and switch it to "Off."** This action will prevent the multiple software firewalls from interfering with each other. In Figure 2-7 *Windows Firewall* is switched off.

Additionally, I also suggest that you outright **delete** any unused software firewall from your system. An **exception** for a Microsoft Windows 7-based computer system would be the *Windows Firewall*, which is an integral part of Microsoft Windows 7. I did not delete *Windows Firewall,* **but I switched it off**.

To remove a "3rd party" (non-Microsoft) software firewall from a Microsoft Windows 7 system, click on the "Start" menu button, then "Control Panel," then "Programs and Features." Click on the displayed name of the undesired firewall and follow the resulting "uninstall" instructions.

I will continue to use as this book's demonstration example the software firewall GFI/Sunbelt "Software VIPRE Antivirus Premium" (http://www.vipreantivirus.com/Software/VIPRE-Premium-Antivirus/), which incorporates both firewall and antivirus/antispyware functionality.

2. **OPTIONAL: Download (or Install from purchased CD) your "Software Firewall"**

   If you have selected a *new* PC-based (software) firewall, install the software.

3. **Suggested PC (Software) Firewall Settings**

   a. Use default settings upon installation.

   b. Where available, select your PC firewall's "Simple Mode" displays to avoid constant connection status advisories.

      The alternative - the "Learning Mode" – *constantly* displays connection and other normal status advisories. These constant notations are highly educational, but are also highly distracting and not necessary.

   c. Enable the PC (Software) Firewall General protections as shown in **Figure 2-8**

Figure 2-8. General Software Firewall Settings

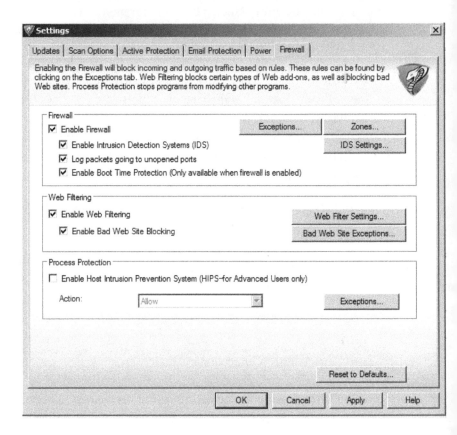

Note the following comments regarding **Figure 2-8:**

   i.   **Enable Firewall** *checked* (of course)

  ii.   **Enable Intrusion Detecton Systems** (IDS) *checked*
       Leave the default settings intact. This will block
       high-risk attempted intrusions.

iii. **Log packets going to unopened ports** *checked.* This will create log (historical) entries for any attempts by hackers trying to access ports your firewall has closed, as during the "port scanning" (surveillance) attacks I mentioned earlier in this chapter.

iv. **Enable Boot Time Protection** *checked.* This will prevent attacks on your individual PC while it is still booting up and you haven't yet logged into your computer with your PC's username/password.

This feature is one example of the reason for installing individual software firewalls on each PC in your network!

v. **Enable Web Filtering** *checked.* This will block certain types of high-risk information from reaching yout Internet browser (i.e. Firefox, Internet Explorer, etc).

NOTE: Some websites will be blocked by Web Filtering. I found that I could not log into my AOL email website.

vi. **Enable Bad Website Blocking** *checked.* This will block "blacklisted" websites that are known to your firewall's software to download, often automatically, hostile virus content.

This feature is one example of the reason your PC's firewall software, as well as all other software, must be updated constantly.

The separate **"Bad Websites Exception"** button, if clicked, will cause a screen to be displayed that will enable you to enter **exceptions to the "Bad Website"** blacklist. DO NOT USE THE "BAD WEBSITES EXCEPTION" UTILITY UNLESS YOU ARE CONDUCTING SECURITY TESTS OF POTENTIALLY HOSTILE WEBSITES.

vii. **Host Intrusion Detection System** *unchecked*

This very powerful utility, which monitors all dynamic system behavior, will require frequent exceptions being added by the User (you). *One exception I was required to add was to permit downloading technical documents!* I don't recommend this option unless you are prepared to frequently edit the **Host Intrusion Detection System.**

4. **Click on the Software Firewall Protections "Exceptions" Button to Block File Transfer Protocol ("FTP," Ports 20 and 21)**

Unless FTP is needed on your PC for updating personal websites, downloading software, or supporting corporate file systems, I suggest you add FTP to the list of blocked services. To block FTP create a so-called "Firewall Exceptions/**Port Rule**" in your PC (software) firewall. In **Figure 2-9** note that I have selected **Port 20** (FTP Data) as being "blocked with notify." (This is because you *do* want to be notified if an unauthorized FTP transfer is attempted, either accidentally or by a hostile entity).

NOTE: An identical procedure is required for **Port 21** (FTP *Control* signals).

Figure 2-9. Block FTP Using Your Specially Created Software Firewall "Port Rule"

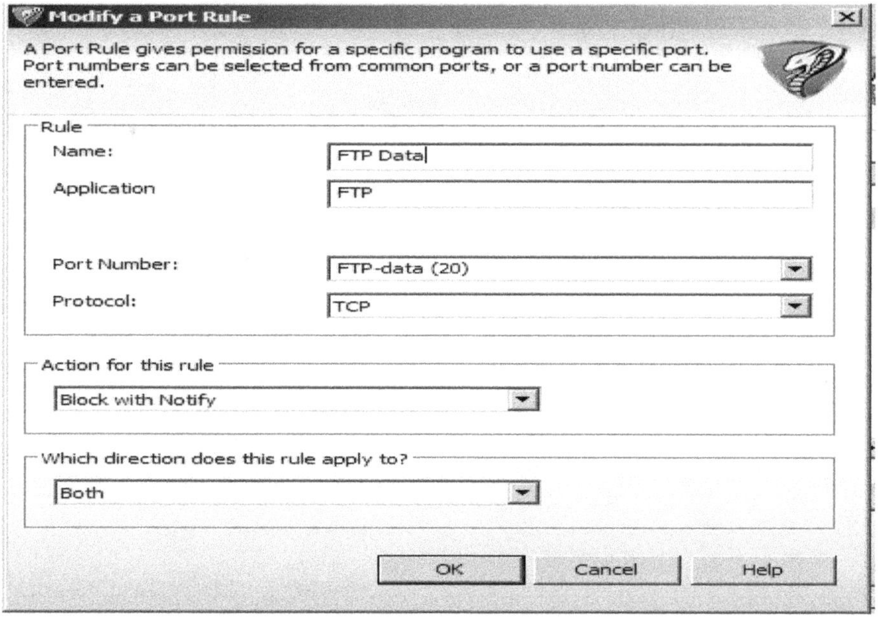

Then click on "**OK**"

Next we must adjust the software firewall's **Web Filter Settings** in order to further improve our security configuration.

Click on the **Web Filter Settings** button. The filter settings screen will then be displayed, as shown in **Figure 2-9**.

Figure 2-9. Suggested Firewall Web Filter Settings

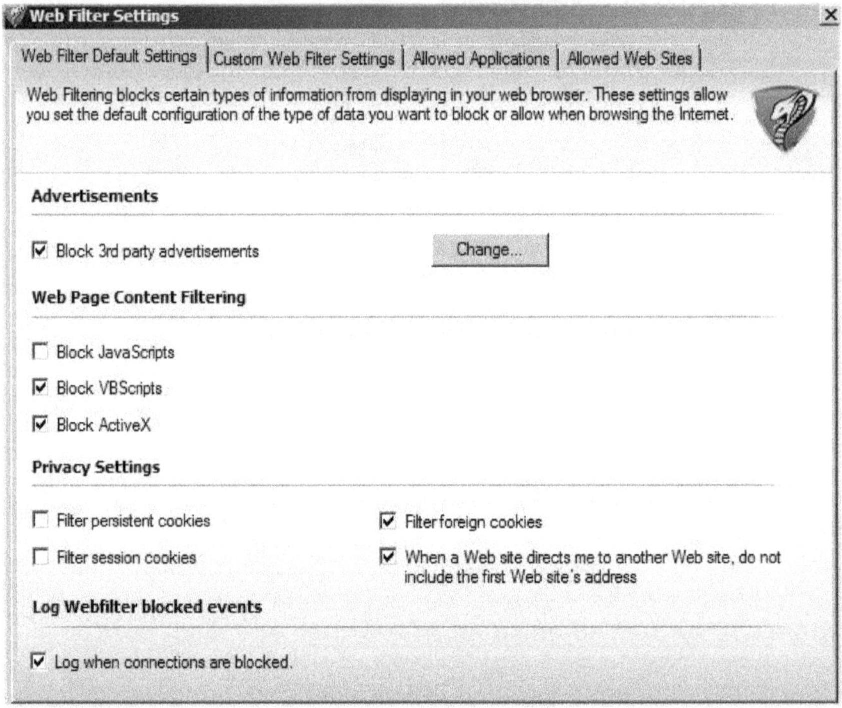

Note the following comments regarding **Figure 2-9:**

i. **Block 3rd party advertisements** *checked*. This will block website ads from additional "3rd parties" that often, in addition to being annoying, are often not always *directly* related to the subject matter you want to view. These ads needlessly consume your PC's video resources.

ii.   **Block JavaScripts** *unchecked.* This will permit website JavaScripts to run on your PC. JavaScripts are required for *so many* websites, including legitimate Web-based forms and video displays such as those in YouTube, that I suggest allowing them to run.

NOTE: Corporations sometimes restrict JavaScript functions to prevent employees from online shopping and other activities requiring JavaScript.

In addition, JavaScripts are sometimes used by hackers to deliver harmful content.

iii.   **Block VB Scripts** *checked.* This will prevent VB Script downloads from the Web, many of which are used to deliver hostile content, often **as email attachments** with ".vbs" filenames. Sometimes the hostile VB Script (.vbs file) is concealed within yet *another* type of file – the ".zip" or "ZIP" file, which stores and hides a file or group of files in a compressed container.

iv.   **Block ActiveX** *checked.* This will prevent downloads of so-called "Active X" files, which are small – and often very powerful – computer programs. Hostile ActiveX downloads have been used by hackers to deliver destructive computer virus content to Web Users' PCs.

NOTE: Some legitmate software programs will *require that you download and install an ActiveX program* so that you may install or update your purchase!

In addition, many legitimate programs that may reside on your PC, such as Microsoft MS Office, are themselves ActiveX software components. Upgrading these software components may require that you permit the ActiveX download by clicking on an new authorization button (i.e. "Click to Allow ActiveX download") suddenly displayed in your Internet browser by the vendor.

v. **Filter session cookies** *unchecked.* "Cookies" are small blocks of information created by websites you visit. "Session" cookies reside only in your computer's microchip memory. Many password-protected websites require session cookies to "remember" that you have logged into the site, allowing you to visit multiple Web pages on the site *for the duration of your Web browser session.* They are erased *when your PC's Web browser is closed.* **For this reason many banking and finance websites display a message instructing you to close your Web browser once you have logged out.**

One of the most frequent causes of my clients being unable to log into a password-protected site is that their session cookies have been "turned off" or restricted.

I suggest that you set your software (PC-based) firewall to allow (**not** "filter") session-based cookies, to facilitate your logging into password-protected websites.

vi. **Filter persistent cookies** *unchecked.*
Persistent (long-term) cookies store website **username, password**, marketing, and other

information, such as your website appearance preferences when visiting the site, *in small text files on your PC's hard drive*. This data truly *is* persistent, with default cookie "expiration" dates often extending years into the future! **This represents a security risk.**

Unfortunately, some of the older password-protected websites **require persistent cookies** to "remember" that you have logged into the site, allowing you to access website utilities and pages *you* are authorized for. This enables you to utilize these approved website capabilities *for the duration of your Web browser website login session.* For this reason I suggest that you set your software (PC-based) firewall to allow (**not** "filter") persistent cookies, to facilitate your logging into websites that still require them. NOTE: Corporations sometimes restrict persistent cookies because of the potential security (**username/password storage**) and privacy risks. This corporate-imposed cookie restriction may prevent employees from logging into certain password-protected websites.

In **Chapter 4** you'll learn how to set your Web browser to allow persistent cookies to be downloaded to your hard drive and then *automatically erase these "persistent" cookies once your Web browser has been closed.*

vii. **Filter foreign cookies** *checked.*
"Foreign," or "3rd party" cookies, also store portions of your website visit experience in small text files on your PC's hard drive. Foreign cookies are placed on your system by 3rd party websites that

have contributed content (usually legitimately) to the "main" website you are visiting.

3rd party content is used very often on the Internet. Most well-known news websites, for example, use 3rd party content from other news sources that invisibly blends with the Web page you have selected. These "other" sites often place cookies on your PC to gather additional marketing information, which represent a potential privacy risk.

I suggest that you set your software (PC-based) firewall to "filter" 3rd party cookies.

If certain password-protected websites require 3rd party cookies to support user login, I have found it effective to set my Web browser to accept them. In addition to being restricted by your software firewall, cookies are also restricted by Web browser settings on your PC. Examples of Web browser cookie settings are described in **Chapter 4.**

NOTE: Corporations sometimes restrict "foreign" 3rd party cookies because of the potential privacy risk.

Configuring Your System to Improve Network Security

Block "Remote Assistance/Remote Control" Utility

I suggest that you do not allow your computer to be accessed or controlled remotely unless this becomes absolutely necessary. Necessary exceptions include troubleshooting essential connections to your Internet Service Provider ("**ISP**") or a corporate network ("**VPN**" or Virtual Private Network) as you interact online with a support technician.

Once the technician's remote support activity is complete, I suggest you disable the "Remote Assistance/Remote Control" utility.

Using Microsoft Windows 7 as an example, click on the "Start" menu button, then "Control Panel," then "System," then the "System Protection" menu link, then the "Remote" tab. As shown in **Figure 2-10**, disable Remote Assistance by *un*checking the "Allow Remote Assistance connections to this computer" checkbox.

Figure 2-10. Disable Remote Control of Your PC

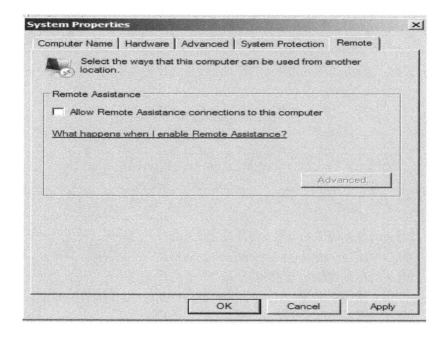

This concludes our discussion of how to configure both types of firewalls – "hardware" (Router-based) and "software" (installed on each PC).

The next chapter will present *more* protection for your computer network. I will describe how we further monitor the Internet data allowed through the firewall's portals that we have allowed to stay "open." In order to maintain our computer system's security, we have to block one of the computer criminal's deadliest software weapons : *malware*.

Chapter 3

Stopping Malware

Viruses, Trojans, Worms, Rootkits, Spyware, and Botnet Sleepers

I ignored Anti Virus because of the cost,
And soon all my data appeared to be lost.
My PC was crippled, unable to boot,
And bank accounts shifted to hacker's loot,
So my personal computer had to be tossed.

Glenn G. Jacobs, geek poet

In **Chapter 2** we discussed how Routers and Firewalls protect your computer network by allowing only a certain few required data portals (out of the potential 65,536) to remain open, while blocking hostile "Port Scanning" surveillance, "Denial of Service"(DoS) attacks, ActiveX threats, and "cookie" web surfing privacy risks.

Firewall protection is absolutely essential. Unfortunately, due to the security risks associated with the Internet, we need an additional protective product.

Let's consider the example of a data portal that is often absolutely necessary and is consequently left "open" (accessible) by many firewalls: Port 110. This port is often used for *incoming* email to your PC. Unfortunately, Port 110 might also deliver hostile, destructive computer virus content (so-called *"malware"*) in addition to legitimate email information. In fact, "corrupt" emails are a primarily vehicle used by criminals to deliver computer viruses to your PC.

In addition to stealing information from your PC, malware can tremendously slow performance to the point of rendering your computer useless. Intolerably slow performance potentially caused by malware is a frequent complaint that I am called to remedy.

For this reason, another security component is required to protect your computer system: *Anti-Virus* (AV) software.

AV software's function is to constantly inspect the streams of incoming and outgoing data allowed by your hardware (Router-based) and software (PC-based) firewalls.

AV software also incorporates an associated essential function, **antispyware**, which specifically prevents the **spyware** type of malware from collecting your personal information and transmitting it to criminal computer networks.

Below is a list of the types of computer malware and how they are often delivered to your PC.

Viruses is the general name for **malware** (software that attacks your PC). During an earlier century, viruses were often designed to totally stop your PC from functioning (for example, to stop your PC from booting up or running essential programs) or to display annoying messages. In today's world, the primary virus purpose is to steal financial and other information – to function as **spyware**. Viruses are delivered by hiding within other vehicles, such as word processor documents, spreadsheets, photo files, videos, and corrupt email messages.

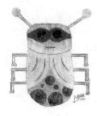

Worms are computer viruses that, after delivery, crawl through networks automatically *without User interaction* and automatically reproduce themselves. Twitter accounts have been used by cyber criminals to transmit worms.

Rootkit malware can seize control of the computer's entire *operating system*, acting as an evil administrator for the PC or network that has been attacked. Rootkits, like most malware, have as their main purpose the theft (or destruction) of sensitive information. In some cases, rootkit malware is used to attack the system's *firmware* - computer code stored in the microchips. Rootkits thus have the somewhat unique ability to interfere with the hardware functions of a PC or network. Rootkits are delivered by corrupt email links in "spam" messages, as well as via infected websites.

In order to prevent their systems from being infected with this very powerful, insidious form of malware, Users should verify that their chosen AV software can detect and eliminate rootkits.

Trojans, functioning like their ancient Greek military "Trojan Horse" namesake, are disguised viruses that appear as legitimate software downloads or email attachments. Once the unfortunate User downloads the corrupt software or clicks on a link in a corrupt email, the Trojan is installed on the User's PC. Many Trojans begin "logging" (recording) the User's keystrokes during credit card or other financial transactions. The Trojan then transmits the financial information to criminal computer networks. This is often done using **FTP** (File Transfer Protocol, PC ports **20** and **21**, which we suggested in **Chapter 2** that you block using your hardware and software firewalls).

Another mysterious criminal use for Trojan viruses is to turn your PC into a "bot," or "zombie," which awaits commands from the criminal **C&C (Command & Control)** center often located thousands of miles away. Your PC, unfortunately, then becomes part of a horde of infected PCs called a "Botnet." The *initial delivery and command/control/communications* mechanism for the Botnet Trojan viruses is often Internet Relay Chat (IRC)

 IRC, as the name implies, enables free "chatroom" communications across the Internet. IRC became popular during the late-1980s and is still widely in use today. Although the majority of IRC networks (and their Users) are pefectly legitimate, the majority of IRC connections are *unencrypted*, leaving IRC networks susceptible to monitoring and attack.

Many corporations block IRC from their networks because of security risks such as inadvertent Botnet Trojan virus downloads. I recommend, as I suggested in **Chapter 2**, you block *the IRC service* (**Port 6667**), unless IRC is specifically required for your home/ business.

After the Botnet **Trojan** is downloaded to your PC, what does it do? **IT SLEEPS!**

Hi ! I'm a sleeping Botnet virus, waiting for my criminal C&C (Command & Control) center to contact me.

Often the sleeping" Botnet" virus is not detected by the User unless they run scans using frequently updated AV software! Their PC may seem to run normally while infected. In other cases, the User may notice an unacceptable slowdown in performance after Botnet infection.

Once the distant criminal **C&C (Command & Control)** center signals your infected PC, the Bot virus "wakes up."

Hi! I'M AWAKE NOW!

Now I can deliver millions of hostile data packets to whatever victim is dictated by my C&C center.

One of the primary purposes of Botnets is 21st-century blatant *extortion.* Your PC, along with thousands of other unwilling members of the "Botnet," could be used to deliver tens of millions of hostile data packets to corporations or financial institutions whose networks are then impaired or even "crashed."

This attack is called a **DDoS** (*Distributed* Denial-of-Service) attack, because the "enemy" (source of hostile clogging data packets) is, sadly, you ☹ and thousands of other innocent people whose PCs are infected with the Botnet virus.

Botnets are also used extensively for political harassment.

Your AV/antispyware software is thus required to **scan your email file downloads, downloaded applications and documents, hard drives, CDs, DVDs, and those popular USB "memory sticks," and then detect, isolate (quarantine), and delete all malware.**

This is no small undertaking. There are upwards of 100,000 new or modified computer viruses released into the Internet each day. For this reason some Users run two or more AV programs at the same time (not recommended), in the hope that at least one program will halt the latest round of evil malware attempting to install itself on their PC. However, *a duplication problem exists*: the multiple AV software products each contain an inspection *and* virus-removal engine named "Automatic Protection" (**AP**), sometimes called "Monitoring." If more than one Antivirus AP service is running, the AP services will interfere with each other and neutralize their effectiveness.

For this reason I suggest not using more than one antivirus/antispyware program at a time.

We will use as this book's demonstration example the software product "VIPRE Antivirus Premium" (http://www.vipreantivirus.com/Software/VIPRE-Premium-Antivirus/), which incorporates both antivirus/antispyware and firewall functionality.

Stopping Malware in Order to Improve Network Security

1. **GETTING STARTED: Verify if any multiple installed AV Software packages are present on your PC**

NOTE: *Never **run** two or more **AV programs (PC-based)** that have their Active Protection (AP) services running at the same time.* These will conflict with each other.

As part of my "cleanup" procedures, I frequently am required to remove or partly disable multiple vendors' versions of **AV software** from my client's PCs in order to stop or prevent these Active Protection conflicts.

To view which AV software is installed and running, I will use a Microsoft Windows 7 example. Click on the "Start" menu button, then "Control Panel," then the "Action Center." As shown in **Figure 3-1**, click on the Security tab down arrow:

Figure 3-1. Click on Security tab down arrow

As shown in **Figure 3-2**, the "View installed antispyware programs" link will appear. Click on this link.

Figure 3-2. Click on "View installed Antispyware"

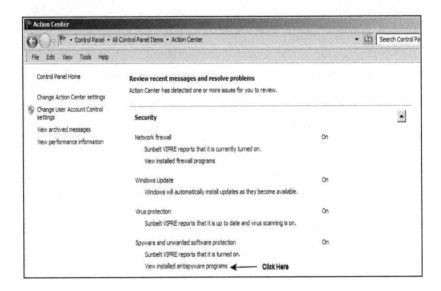

The list of installed antispyware programs will be displayed, along with their **Status** (Off/On). In our example, two antispyware programs have been installed, but, (as required), only one antispyware program (Sunbelt VIPRE) is "On" (running), as shown in **Figure 3-3**.

Figure 3-3. List of Installed Antispyware Programs and their On/Off Status

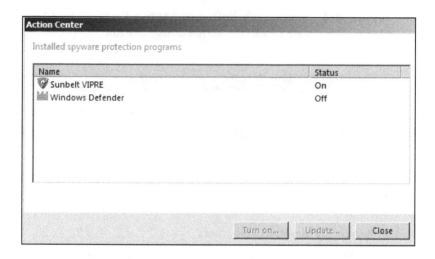

If more than one antispyware software is shown as "On" (running), **click on the link to the undesired antispyware and switch it to "Off."** This action will prevent the multiple AV programs' antispyware functions from interfering with each other. In **Figure 3-3** *Windows Defender* antispyware is switched off.

Additionally, I also suggest that you outright **delete** any unused antispyware from your system. An **exception** for a Microsoft Windows 7-based computer system would be *Windows Defender*, which is an integral part of Microsoft Windows 7. **Do not delete** *Windows Defender.*

To remove a "3rd party" (non-Microsoft) antispyware software product from a Microsoft Windows 7 system, click on the "Start" menu button, then "Control Panel," then "Programs and Features." Click on the displayed name of the undesired firewall and follow the resulting "uninstall" instructions:

2. Enable Active Protection on your AV Software

As shown in **Figure 3-4**, enable the "Active Protection" feature on your AV software so as to prevent the malware from ever infecting your PC.

Figure 3-4. Enable AV Software "Active Protection" (AP) and Click on "Extensions" Button

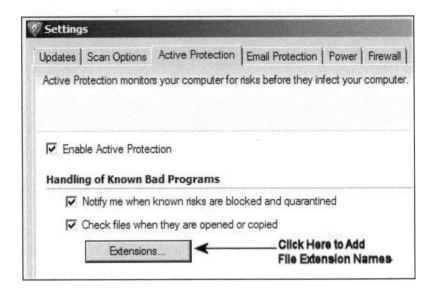

Note that **Figure 3-4** shows the following AV (Antivirus/Antispyware) configuration decisions:

    i. **Enable Active Protection** *checked* (of course). Always purchase AV software that includes Active Protection. **This must include inspection of downloaded email attachments. Sometimes the "free" version of popular AV software does not include the necessary Active Protection "engine."**

    ii.   **Notify me (User) when known risks are blocked and quarantined** *checked.*

This will make the User (you) informed as to corrupted email messages or tainted websites trying to download viruses to your system.

iii.   **Check files when they are opened or copied** *checked.*

In many cases, infected files will not show their virus hostile "behavior" until the file is either opened or copied. For example, one client's company received bogus resumes as word processing documents infected with a virus that shut down their Web server. After I installed Antivirus/antispyware software, the AV report showed that the virus attack began upon **opening** the infected file.

Another similar risk exists with "compressed" files such as those that end in ".ZIP" (so-called **zip** files). File compression is a long-standing legitimate technique, and the use of **zip** files enabled home and business Users to transmit groups of large, cumbersome files over the previous century's slow "dialup" Internet connections. Once the **zip** files arrived at their destination, the recipient User would run their *de*compressing (**un**zip) utility, which would automatically and conveniently extract the original file content to their PC.

Unfortunately, hackers soon learned to place viruses within **zip** files and send them as email messages all over the Web. By deceptive email messages ("phishing email attacks"), Users would be tricked into clicking on the **zip** file, which would then automatically (and **in**conveniently) deliver the virus content to the victim's PC.

NOTE: Corporations sometimes prohibit **zip** files from being received or transmitted via corporate email messages, due to the security risk.

For this reason, I suggest that you click on the "**Extensions**" button shown in **Figure 3-4** above. This will cause the Automatic Protection "AP File Extensions" screen to be displayed, as shown in **Figure 3-5.**

Figure 3-5. Add "ZIP" Files to File Extensions to Be Monitored by Your AV Software

As shown in **Figure 3-5**, click on the "Add" button, and type the expression **ZIP** to cause the AV software to monitor **zip** files and

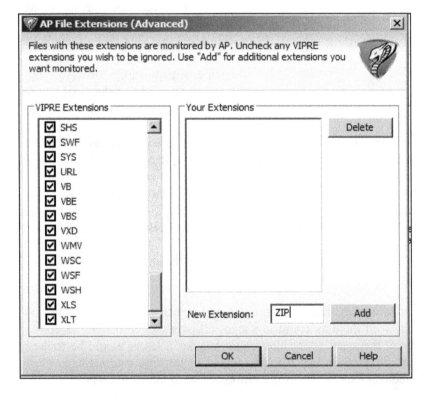

suppress any virus content once these files are opened. Note that your AV software, as shown in **Figure 3-5,** already may have a substantial standard list of files that are always being monitored.

Add any other filename extension (**PDF** for Adobe Portable Data Format files, for example) that you use frequently.

Then, click on "**OK**"

3. Constantly Update Your AV Software

Set your AV software updates to "automatic." This way your PC's Antivirus/Antispyware software will receive the latest virus threat information that your vendor has available to them.

4. Constantly Update Your Operating System Software

Always update your Operating System ("OS"), be it MS Windows, Linux, or Apple Mac OS X, with the newest security update software. These free updates help minimize the possibility of an attack against your system.

5. Scan your Hard Drives Automatically Every Day

Set your AV automatic software scanning schedule to the following:

        a.   Quick Scan (approximately 6 p.m. every day)

        b.   Full ("Deep") Scan (once a week)

Review your AV report logs in order to become acquainted with what times your system may have been under attack.

Was it during email activity? Was it while you were in a chat room?

6. Scan all Documents / Photos / Videos Provided to You on CD/DVD

Every time you receive a CD or DVD containing documents, photos, or video files, immediately perform a scan of its content with your AV software.

 Your friends or coworkers may accidentally be handing you infected files if their PC has been infected.

7. Scan All USB "Memory Sticks"

Many people consider the ubiquitous "Memory Stick" storage device, which plugs into and communicates with your PC via a USB (Universal Serial Bus) connector, to be indispensible. They "install themselves automatically," and provide a convenient, inexpensive backup mechanism.

USB MEMORY STICKS ARE A SECURITY RISK!
SCAN THEM UPON FIRST USE AND AFTER EVERY USE!

 Memory sticks, an example of which is shown in **Figure 3-6**, are often manufactured offshore by entities who may install spyware in the memory chips they contain.

In addition, computer criminals have been known to deliberately place Memory sticks infected with their evil personalized spyware ☹ in coffee shops, corporate kitchens and break rooms, lobbies, and even parking lots. Unknowing Users have picked these Memory sticks up and plugged them into their PCs. Devastating security breaches have resulted.

IT HAS HAPPENED, AND SYSTEMS WERE COMPROMISED!

**Figure 3-6 Memory Stick
with USB Connector**

- You should perform an Antivirus/Antispyware scan on USB memory sticks immediately after purchase.

- Scan with AV after each usage (Backup/Copy, etc.).

8. UPDATE Your Adobe Portable Data Format (PDF) Reader Frequently

 Adobe Portable Data Format (PDF) documents, once not

considered to be a vehicle for cyber attack, are now a major vehicle for malware delivery. To stop PDFs from delivering malware do the following:

a. Download and install the newest free Adobe Reader software, **Adobe Reader X** from the www.adobe.com/products/reader.html website. Adobe Reader X is designed to suppress malware. By default Adobe Reader X will download updates automatically.

b. Manually update your Adobe Reader X every 4 weeks on your PC by selecting from the top menu "Help," then "Check for Updates."

No discussion of malware would be complete without an example of the primary malware delivery mechanism – **corrupt emails**.

> *Ignoring all warnings from my computer geek,*
> *On one email link, I clicked and took a peek,*
> *Then a virus began to suddenly download*
> *And hostile kilobytes to my PC all flowed*
> *As from my accounts, my money did leak.*

> *Glenn G. Jacobs, geek poet*

We have grown tremendously dependent on electronic mail (email) for both personal and business communications. Yet the majority of computer virus "deliveries" to personal computers occur through email messages, followed closely by infections from the social communication websites.

Fortunately, we can suppress email-based malware delivery if we understand the email attack mechanism. Hostile emails are disguised as helpful or even urgent communications requiring immediate action. The hostile email often represents itself as being sent from a benign institution such as a bank. This type of cyber criminal attack is called a "phishing attack."

For this reason, I included an example of a corrupt email message filled with hostile Trojan virus download links. These links are disguised as legitimate online bank help resources, as shown in

Figure 3-7. To protect the privacy of the recipient I have disguised the "bank institution" name as well as the recipient, and have concealed bank account information.

The "phishing attack" email message shown in **Figure 3-7** is entirely real-life. To evaluate each of the hostile hyperlinks I copied and pasted each of them into a search engine.

I found this "search engine inspection" to be quite helpful in identifying the criminal activity. Not only did each supposedly innocent link suddenly and clearly "change" its value within the search engine textbox from www.yourbank.com to an obvious overseas source of viral downloads. I also discovered that there were numerous complaints from security experts about each of the "phishing attack" hyperlinks.

Figure 3-7. Hostile Email Example with Disguised Trojan
Download Links

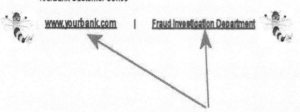

EXAMPLE OF REAL-LIFE "PHISHING" ATTACK EMAIL

From: "YourBank Customer Service" <customerservice@yourbank.com>
To: <your_email_address@email.com>
Sent: By the millions every day
Subject: YourBank Insufficient Funds Notice

Hostile Web Link
to Trojan Virus → www.yourbank.com
Download

Insufficient Funds Notice

Unfortunately, **recently** your available balance in your **checking** account XXXXXXXXX
was insufficient to cover one or more of your checks, Check Card purchases, or other transactions.

An important notice regarding one or more of your payments is now available in your Messages &
Alerts inbox.

To read the message, sign on at **our website,** go to Messages & Alerts, and open the Insufficient
Funds Notice.

Please make deposits to cover your payments, fees, and any other withdrawals or transactions you
have initiated. If you have already taken care of this, please disregard this notice.

We appreciate your business and thank you for your prompt attention to this matter.

If you have questions after reading the notice in your inbox, please refer to the contact information
in the notice. Please do not reply to this automated email.

Sincerely,

YourBank Customer Sevice

www.yourbank.com | **Fraud Investigation Department**

Hostile Web Links to Trojan Virus Downloads

Note the following typical, consistent characteristics of many "phishing attacks."

1. Falsified bank or institutional graphic or logo (not shown here) in order to lure victim to trust the source.

2. Falsified "**From**" identity (falsified email source).

3. Urgent phony **Subject** matter ("**Insufficient Funds Notice**") requiring victim to take immediate action (i.e. click on the disguised hostile Trojan virus download links to "get help").

4. Multiple hostile disguised links (i.e. phony "**Fraud Investigation Department**" link) that will download a Trojan virus. The Trojan is intended to monitor and transmit your keystrokes (as a "**keylogger**" virus) to a criminal computer network. This transfer of your financial information is often done using **FTP** (File Transfer Protocol, PC ports **20** and **21)**, or **IRC** (Internet Relay Chat, PC port **6667**), which was suggested in **Chapter 2** that you block using your hardware and software firewalls.

Note that the key to defeating this type of attack is **the User (you). YOU MAKE THE DECISION NOT TO CLICK ON THE HOSTILE LINKS.**

Unfortunately, **I was also the target of a phishing email attack**. I have included an example of "my" real-life corrupt email message. This time, the bogus email message, filled with *misspellings and horrible grammar*, referred to a non-existent parcel delivery. The Trojan virus was already attached to the hostile email as a **.ZIP** file, waiting for the victim (me) to click on it so the Trojan virus could self-install ☹

My personal phishing email is shown in **Figure 3-8.**

To protect the privacy of the recipient ☺ I have disguised the intended victim's email address. I have also disguised the legitimate parcel delivery corporation's name and "sender" email address.

Figure 3-8. "Phishing" Email Example Showing Trojan Virus Contained within Corrupt ZIP File Attachment

In the next chapter I will describe how to protect your interaction with Web content. My goal is now to protect your Internet "binoculars" – that essential PC software known as the "Web browser."

Chapter 4

Browser & Web Surfing Security

I opened up my browser and frequently did surf,
Forgetting all security, of which there was a dearth
With the browser displaying just what I wished to see,
While viruses were downloaded to my new PC
Resulting in data leaks which were then given birth.

Glenn G. Jacobs, geek poet

What is a Web Browser?

A Web browser is a computer program that enables the User (you) to view and interact with Internet websites. Browsers reside on each desktop or laptop PC (client) in your network, and are thus called "client" software.

Two popular browsers include *Firefox* (Mozilla Foundation, www.mozilla.com/en-US/firefox) and *Internet Explorer* (Microsoft Corporation, http://windows.microsoft.com/en-us/internet-explorer/download/ie-9/worldwide).

Browsers act as your "portal" to the incredible World Wide Web. Users access websites by typing in the Internet address (URL) in the "address box" located near the top of the browser. Icons for these two well-known browsers are shown below in **Figure 5-1** and **Figure 5-2,** respectively.

Figure 5-1
Firefox icon

Figure 5-2
Internet Explorer icon

Unfortunately, the browser is also a primary mechanism for computer virus attack because of its connection to the Internet.

This chapter will use Firefox version **3.6** configuration settings and snapshots to illustrate our concepts for reducing browser security risks.

Configuring Your Firefox Browser to Improve Computer Security:

To access your Firefox settings, click on "Tools" then "Options" for MS Windows systems (For Linux systems click on "Edit" then "Preferences"). Using the Firefox browser as an example, I am listing suggested security-related settings below that apply to all Internet Web browsers. Firefox settings are divided into **tabs**.

  1. General tab (**Figure 5-3**)

  a.   When Firefox starts *Show my home page.*

In addition to being a convenience for your work online, this setting provides an obvious warning if your Web browser has been "hijacked" (reprogrammed to point to a new home page).

Some legitimate software products, after installation, alter your Web browser's settings to display a home page website other than your originally chosen selection. In most cases, the new "home page" simply displays legitimate product information and, predictably, more advertising for the vendor every time you start your browser. In these cases, the User (you) can immediately set the Web browser back to your original choice.

In the case of a virus attack, your Web browser home page setting may be changed to display a website with objectionable or even illicit content. In most cases, the User will not be able to change the browser home page setting at all, despite repeated editing attempts. Should your Web browser home page be "hijacked," I suggest you do the following immediately:

    i.   Run a full Antivirus (AV) scan on your PC and delete any malware detected. Then change your browser home page back to your personal choice and reboot your PC.

    ii. If the AV scan is not effective, I suggest you download and install another AV package named **Malwarebytes**. A free version is available from www.malwarebytes.org. After installing **Malwarebytes**, use it to run a full AV scan on your PC and delete any malware detected. Then change your browser home page back to your personal choice and reboot your PC.

       Malwarebytes has been shown to be particularly highly effective in remedying "hijacking" attacks on Web browser home pages and also in removing so-called "extortionware," where the User is denied access to certain file folders unless the User pays online for "removal."

b.   **Home Page.** Enter the Web page you wish to view upon startup. Suggested home pages might be search engines, classroom Web pages, or news websites.

c.   **Manage Add-ons.** "Add-ons" and "Plugins" are software packages that enable the Web User to perform extra tasks, such as viewing audio/video displays or completing forms online. **Frequently updating your commonly used Web browser Plugins is essential to maintaining your PCs security.**

Click on the **Manage Add-ons** button and to verify that you have installed and updated the following Plugins:

i. Adobe Flash Player (displays Web "Flash" animations and advertisements, and facilitates some password login forms, in your browser). Some Flash animations have been corrupted by cyber criminals, requiring frequent Flash Player security updates. (www.adobe.com/go/getflashplayer)

ii. Adobe PDF Reader Plugin (displays Web-based Adobe Portable Data Format (PDF) documents in your browser). Some PDFs have been corrupted by cyber criminals, requiring frequent Adobe PDF reader Plugin security updates. (http://get.adobe.com/reader)

iii. Java (facilitates some password login forms and a few Web animations in your browser). Some Java Web downloads ("applets") have been corrupted by cyber criminals. It is essential that you frequently update your Java applet-running software (so-called **JRE**, "Java Runtime Environment) with the latest version http://java.com/en/download/

To test your Java **JRE** functionality visit the below URL: www.java.com/en/download/testjava.jsp

iv. Apple QuickTime (facilitates audio-visual Web displays in your browser). Some QuickTime downloads have been corrupted by cyber criminals. It is essential that you frequently update your Apple QuickTime Plugin: www.apple.com/quicktime/download

IT IS ESSENTIAL THAT YOU FREQUENTLY UPDATE ALL BROWSER PLUGINS IN ORDER TO BENEFIT FROM SECURITY UPGRADES. MANY OF THESE PLUGINS ARE "3RD PARTY," WHICH INCREASES THE POTENTIAL

REQUIREMENT FOR MORE SECURITY SCRUTINY ON THE PART OF THE USER.

The Firefox Third Party Plugin Description/Update list is available at: https://www.mozilla.com/en-US/plugincheck/

Figure 5-3. "General" Firefox Browser Options Tab

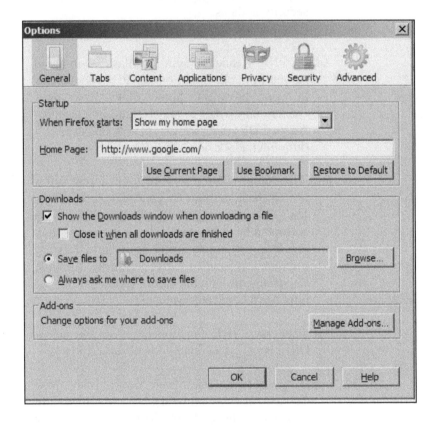

2. Content tab **(Figure 5-4)**

    a.   **Block pop-up windows** *checked.*

So-called "pop-up" windows are usually legitimate but annoying vehicles for dumping additional advertising content in front of the User (you). In some cases, pop-up windows have contained displays of and solicitation for illicit material. I suggest you block pop-up windows.

However, some online purchase pages, online tutorial pages, or software installation Web pages may require pop-ups to be authorized by you. In this case, a small button labeled "Allow Pop-ups for this Website" will appear near the top of your Web browser for you to click on.

b. Load images automatically *checked.*

Images add clarity to Web pages, and speed our comprehension with graphs and diagrams. Unfortunately, cyber criminals have been able to add hostile content to some graphical files. The User (you) can restrict graphics downloads to only those websites you trust by clicking on the "**Exceptions**" button (next to the **Load images automatically** checkbox) and entering the website addresses you want images from.

c. Enable JavaScript *checked.*

JavaScript is required by so many websites to load graphical/video objects that I suggest you allow your browser to run these scripts. For example, many 'Flash" animations, such as those in YouTube, cannot be displayed in your browser without JavaScript.

Unfortunately, cyber criminals have been able to launch hostile content using JavaScript. The User (you) can restrict JavaScript functions to only those websites you trust by clicking on the "**Exceptions**" button (next to the **Enable JavaScript** checkbox) and entering the websites you wish JavaScript enabled for.

Figure 5-4. "Content" Firefox Browser Options Tab

3. Privacy tab **(Figure 5-5)**

   a. HISTORY: Firefox will *Use custom settings for history.*

Since your Web browsing history sessions are a potential target for cyber criminals, I suggest you customize how historical browsing data is stored.

    i. **Remember my browsing history for 90 days** *checked.*

This choice is my compromise between *no* storage (which may be inconvenient) of browsing history and permanent storage. Note that some corporations flat out do not permit storage of browsing history or urge Users to erase the history.

ii **Remember download history** *checked.*

This choice will store a list of your downloaded software and documents, which will probably prove to be an indispensible convenience.

iii **Remember search and form history** *unchecked !!!!!!*

NEVER STORE YOUR COMPLETED FORM INFORMATION, **ESPECIALLY USERNAMES AND PASSWORDS**, ON YOUR PC! USERNAMES AND PASSWORDS ARE A PRIMARY CYBER CRIMINAL INFORMATION TARGET!

iv **Accept cookies from sites** *checked.*

"Cookies" are small blocks of information created by websites you visit. "Session" cookies reside only in your computer's microchip memory. Many password-protected websites require session cookies to "remember" that you have logged into the site, allowing you to visit multiple Web pages on the site *for the duration of your Web browser session.* They are erased *when your PC's Web browser is closed.* **For this reason many banking and finance websites display a message instructing you to close your Web browser once you have logged out.**

I suggest that you set your software browser to accept cookies, to facilitate your logging into password-protected websites.

v. **Keep until** *I close Firefox.*
Persistent (long-term) cookies store website

username, password, marketing, and other information, such as your website appearance preferences when visiting the site, *in small text files on your PC's hard drive.* This data truly *is* persistent, with default cookie "expiration" dates often extending years into the future! **This represents a security risk.**

Unfortunately, some of the older password-protected websites **require persistent cookies** to "remember" that you have logged into the site, allowing you to access website utilities and pages *you* are authorized for. This enables you to utilize these approved website capabilities *for the duration of your Web browser website login session.* For this reason I suggest that you set your browser to accept **persistent** cookies, to facilitate your logging into websites that still require them.

NOTE: Corporations sometimes restrict persistent cookies because of the potential security (**username/password storage**) and privacy risks.

This corporate-imposed cookie restriction may prevent employees from logging into certain password-protected websites.

The "**Keep until** *I close Firefox*" security selection *automatically erases these "persistent" cookies once your Web browser has been closed.*

> vi. **Accept 3rd party cookies** *checked ONLY IF NEEDED FOR WEBSITE LOGIN*

"Foreign", or "3rd party" cookies, also store portions of your website visit experience in small text files on your PC's hard drive. 3rd party cookies are placed on your system by 3rd party websites that have contributed content (usually legitimately) to the "main" website you are visiting.

3rd party content is used very often on the Internet. Most well-known news websites, for example, use 3rd party content from other news sources that invisibly blends with the Web page you have selected. These "other" sites often place cookies on your PC to gather additional marketing information, which represent a potential privacy risk.

I suggest that you set your browser to accept 3rd party cookies *only if certain password-protected websites require them to support user login.*

NOTE: Corporations sometimes restrict "foreign" 3rd party cookies because of the potential privacy risk.

Figure 5-5. "Privacy" Firefox Browser Options Tab

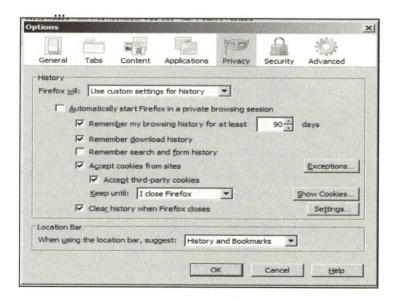

Click on the **Settings button,** and configure your settings as shown in **Figure 5-6**.

Figure 5-6 . Suggested Privacy "Settings" for Firefox Browser

4. Security tab **(Figure 5-7)**

    a. **Warn me when sites try to install add-ons** *checked.*

I suggest you require your Web browser to always require your approval before installing one of those powerful add-on "plug-in" software programs.

    b. **Block reported attack sites** *checked.*

Any website reported to be downloading virus content should be blocked. There are causes where the additional suspect website examination required here has apparently slowed performance. As a result, some Users have chosen to leave this box unchecked.

    c. **Block reported web forgeries** *checked.*

There are causes where the additional suspect website examination required here has apparently slowed performance. As a result, some Users have chosen to leave this box unchecked.

    c. **Remember passwords for sites** *unchecked.*

NEVER STORE ANY USERNAMES AND PASSWORDS, ON YOUR PC!   USERNAMES AND PASSWORDS ARE A PRIMARY CYBER CRIMINAL INFORMATION TARGET!

Figure 5-7. "Security" Firefox Browser Options Tab

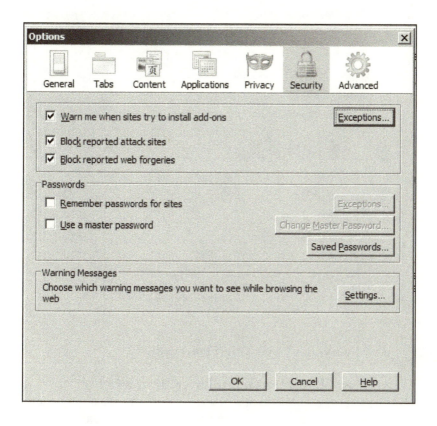

5. **Advanced** tab (**Figure 5-8**)

Three "sub-tabs" underneath the Firefox Options "**Advanced**" tab are security-related, as shown in **Figure 5-8.**

Figure 5-8. "Advanced" Firefox Browser Tab with Sub-Tabs

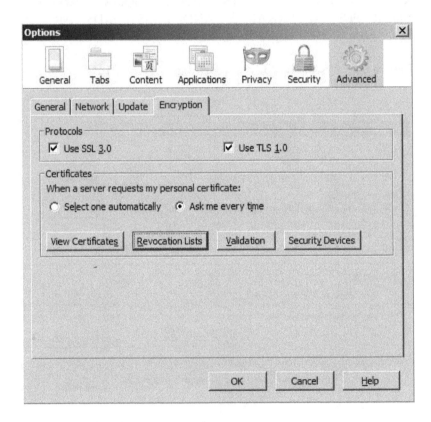

a. **"Encryption" Sub-Tab (Figure 5-8)**

i. **Use SSL (Secure Sockets Layer) 3.0** *checked.*
SSL technology "encrypts" your browser data (converts transmission to a form unreadable to unauthorized readers). Almost all online credit card transactions require "SSL version 3.0" as of this writing.

ii. **Use TLS (Transport Layer Security) 1.0** *checked.*
TLS technology further improves the encrypted transmission security by resisting message tampering.

The combination of **SSL3.0/TLS/1.0** is currently considered the best commercial browser encryption protocol for Web data transmission.

iii. **Certificates – When a Server Requests my Personal Certificate** *Ask me every time (checked).*

Your browser's security certificate file, stored on your PC's hard drive, identifies your PC – and, of course, *you.*

Whenever a website requests your personal (PC) security certificate, *you* should make the decision regarding the website's validity. *You can, for example, enter the website's URL in a search engine to determine if there have been any security complaints.*

b. **"Update" Sub-Tab (Figure 5-9)**

i. **Automatically check for updates:** Firefox *checked*, Add-ons *checked*, Search Engines *checked.*

Updating your software is a key element of maintaining your PC's security.

ii. **When updates to Firefox are found:** Automatically download and install the updates *checked.*

iii. **Warn me if this will disable any of my add-ons (plugins)** *checked.*

Automatic Firefox updates offer convenience to the User. The User should be warned if the new Firefox version installation will disable any of the already installed "add-ons" (plugins), such as audio/video playback software.

86

Figure 5-9. Firefox "Update" Sub-Tab

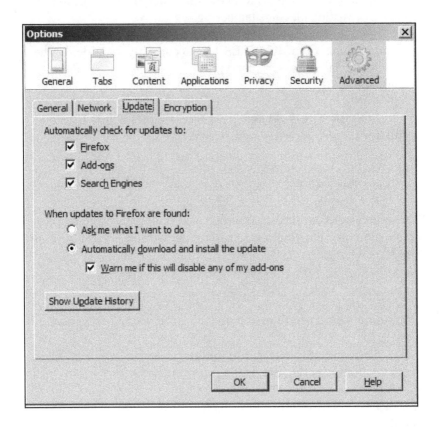

c. **"Network" Sub Tab (Figure 5-10)**

i. **Tell me when a website asks to store data for offline use** *checked.*

Whenever a website requests to store information on your PC, *you should make the decision regarding the website's validity. You can, for example, enter the website's URL in a search engine to determine if there have been any security complaints.*

Figure 5-10. Firefox "Network" Sub-Tab

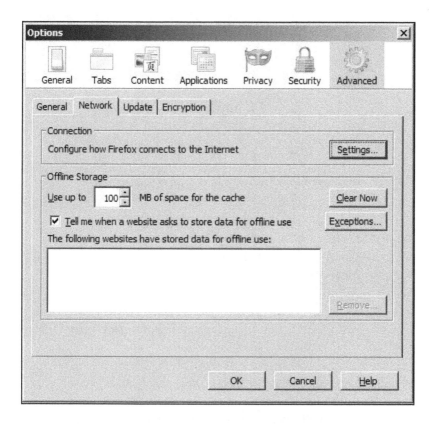

This completes our chapter on **Browser & Web Surfing Security.** The next and final chapter will summarize the computer security concepts presented in this book.

Chapter 5

Computer Security Summary

Protect Your Computer from Cyber Attack !

Remember the risks, they're yours to control,
Security always must be your goal,
Forgetfulness once can cost tons of cash,
Not to mention that your whole system can crash.

Glenn G. Jacobs, geek poet

Wireless Internet ("WiFi") Settings

- Set WiFi Router "Administrative" password to an obscure mixture of 10 uppercase and lowercase alphabetical characters and numbers. Do not use numbers in sequence (i.e. "12345" etc.).
- Set WiFi wireless User login username ("SSID") to an obscure mixture of 10 uppercase and lowercase alphabetical characters and numbers. Do not use numbers in sequence (i.e. "12345" etc.).
- Disable SSID (WiFi username) radio "broadcast" unless required by older laptop or PC operating systems.
- Never use WEP (Wired Equivalency Privacy) WiFi Encryption. It's far too weak.
- Set Your WiFi Encryption "Security Option" to WPA-**2** with AES (Advanced Encryption System).
- Set WiFi wireless User login WPA-**2** "passphrase"

(password) to an obscure mixture of 10 uppercase and lowercase alphabetical characters and numbers. Do not use numbers in sequence (i.e. "12345" etc.).

- Set WiFi Router Software Updates to "Automatic."
- OPTIONAL: Restrict WiFi Network Access to Specific Wireless Computers. If you choose this option, note that you must add/delete PCs/laptops to/from your WiFi Router's internal Wireless Access List every time your authorized WiFi User list changes.
- Disable "Automatic Wireless Connections" (Automatic Login Near Any Wireless Network) except for your Home WiFi system.
- Never connect to Wireless Networks with SSIDs (usernames) such as "Free Public WiFi". These may be "rogue" (criminal) WiFi networks that will steal information from your PC.
- Disable Wireless "Internet Connection Sharing." By default this utility is always "on," causing your PC to become a WiFi "Access Point" (also called a "WiFi Miniport" for MS Windows 7), creating a virtual "Wireless Internet Coffeeshop" inside your PC. This poses a security risk.

General Router-based ("Hardware") Firewall Settings

- Block "Pings" (Surveillance Test Signals) from the Internet, unless required by your corporate Virtual Private Network (VPN).
- Block Port Scan Surveillance.
- Enable "Stateful Packet Inspection" (SPI). SPI examines the incoming packets to ensure that they are part of a "legitimate" connection to your network, and not part of a Denial-of-Service (DoS) attack or Port Scanning attack against your system.
- Block **FTP** (**F**ile **T**ransfer **P**rotocol) unless it is required for updating personal websites, downloading software, or supporting corporate file systems. FTP sends its login username/password as unprotected clear text, and is a

security risk. Computer viruses often transmit stolen information via FTP. Most websites and corporate networks now offer encrypted connections (i.e. Virtual Private Networks or VPNs) as alternatives to minimize data transfer risk.

- Block **IRC (I**nternet **R**elay **C**hat), which is a common vehicle for spreading Trojan viruses that may turn your PC into a "bot" used to attack other PCs.
- Constantly update your hardware (Router-based) firewall "firmware" (software downloaded to the firewall microchips).

General PC-based ("Software") Firewall Settings

- Block **FTP (F**ile **T**ransfer **P**rotocol).
- Block **IRC (I**nternet **R**elay Chat).
- NEVER RUN MORE THAN ONE PC-BASED (SOFTWARE) FIREWALL AT ONE TIME.
- Constantly update your PC-based firewall software.
- Restrict cookies (tracking data) as much as allowed by your password login websites.

Anti-Virus (AV) / Antispyware Settings

- NEVER RUN MORE THAN ONE AV ACTIVE PROTECTION ENGINE AT ONE TIME.
- Always purchase AV/Antispware software that identifies and removes those destructive **rootkit** viruses.
- Update your AV software daily.
- "Quick Scan" your PC every day.
- "Full Scan" your PC at last once a week.
- Scan all documents and photos supplied to you on CDs, DVDs, and those popular USB "memory sticks."

Adobe Portable Data Format (PDF) Files

- Constantly update your Adobe PDF Reader application.

Operating System ("OS") Software Updates

- Constantly download and install updates ("patches") for your operating system ("OS") software. This includes all security updates for Microsoft Windows, Linux, and Apple Mac OS X.

Email Security

- Enable Email inspection by Hardware (Router) and Software (PC) firewalls and AntiVirus (AV) software.
- Enable Email "Active Protection" (instant response/quarantine of computer viruses) for your AntiVirus (AV) software where applicable. Some of the newer AV software does not inspect email content until a file download occurs.
- Never click on "hyperlinks" (links to websites or "document downloads") within an email. Instead, copy the link and paste it into a search engine (such as Google, Bing, Yahoo, etc), followed by the word "complaints." If the link is "hostile" (connected to a criminal website) the search engine will immediately list numerous reports from security people.

Browser/Web Surfing Security

- Never click on holiday or gift season links (i.e. "Did You Forget Valentine's Day?") or unknown catastrophe charity links (i.e. "Please Help The Japanese Tsunami Victims") placed on various websites. Many of these "legally" paid-for links connect to criminal websites.
- Restrict cookies (tracking data) as much as allowed by your password login websites.
- Set your browser to erase *all* the "cookies" (text files supplied by websites) every time the browser is closed.
- Constantly update your browser "add-ons" (plugin software) to help suppress cyber attacks.

Back Up Your Sensitive Data

- Backup your data to a 2 Terabyte (TB) mass storage unit.

Home Office Printer/Copier Disposal

This is the kind of backup you *don't* want ☹

- Retrieve and destroy (or securely store) the hard disk drive data storage elements in office-grade printers and copiers.

REMEMBER....MOST IMPORTANT TO YOUR SECURITY ARE....YOUR EDUCATION AND AWARENESS !!!

Appendix A

Default Router Settings, Related Web Links, and Last Resort Password Reset

In Table A-1 is a **table of default administrative settings** for selected popular Wireless Routers. The default usernames, passwords, and "IP Addresses" (Router Admin Website Addresses) listed in the table will enable the User (with a PC connected to the router via an Ethernet network cable) to login to the router's internal "website" and reconfigure and set security for the network. The default passwords are almost always case-sensitive. In many cases the username is also case sensitive.

To assist you if your Router username/password is not listed in Table A-1, we have included in this Appendix a list of **Related Web Links** that contain searchable lists of additional default router usernames, passwords, and "IP Addresses" for internal Router Admin websites.

Also, in **Appendix B** we have included the procedure for determining the internal Admin IP Address for your router, using your PC.

As mentioned in **Chapter 1**, a large number of routers are installed and left operating with the password set to insecure, easily guessed default values such as "password" or "wireless." Note in Table A-1 the significant number of insecure default usernames and passwords.

IT IS ABSOLUTELY ESSENTIAL TO CHANGE YOUR
ROUTER ADMININSTRATION PASSWORD TO AN OBSCURE
MIXTURE OF LETTERS AND NUMBERS THAT WILL BE
IMPOSSIBLE FOR HACKERS TO GUESS .

 **IMPROPER ROUTER SOFTWARE
SETTINGS MAY ALLOW HACKERS
AND OTHER HOSTILE ENTITIES TO
EASILY BREAK INTO YOUR SYSTEM
AND STEAL PASSWORDS AND OTHER
IMPORTANT DATA !**

Table 5-1. List of Default Wireless Router Admin Settings

ROUTER MANUFACTURER	MODEL	ROUTER ADMIN INTERNAL "WEBSITE" IP ADDRESS	DEFAULT ADMIN USERNAME	DEFAULT ADMIN PASSWORD
2 WIRE	490	192.168.1.254	<blank>	wireless
3COM	(Most models)	192.168.1.1	<blank> or admin	admin or comcomcom
Apple Computer	MC340LL/A Airport Extreme Base Station	192.168.1.1 or 10.0.1.1 or 172.16.1.1	<blank>	admin
Belkin	F5D6130 Wireless Access Point (WAP)	192.168.2.1	<blank>	miniAP
Belkin	Wireless ADSL Modem/Router	192.168.2.1	admin	<blank>
Cisco	AIRONET 1100	10.10.10.1	<blank> or Cisco (case-sensitive)	Cisco (case-sensitive)
D-Link	DIR-601 N-150 Wireless Router	192.168.0.1	admin	<blank>
D-link	DIR-655 Extreme-N Wireless Router	192.168.0.1	admin	<blank>
D-link	D-Link DIR-825 Xtreme N Dual Band Gigabit Router	192.168.0.1	admin	<blank>
Linksys (Cisco)	WRT54GLWireless-G Broadband Router	192.168.1.1	admin	admin
Linksys (Cisco)	WRT160NL Wireless-N Broadband Router	192.168.1.1	admin	admin
Linksys	**(Older Models Only)**	192.168.1.1	<blank>	admin
Motorola	SBG900 Wireless Router	192.168.100.1	admin	motorola
Netgear	DG834G Wireless Router	192.168.0.1	admin	password
Netgear	WGR614 Wireless-G Router	192.168.1.1 or 192.168.0.1	admin	password
Netgear	WNDR3700 Wireless Router	192.168.1.1	admin	password

Netgear	WNR2000 Wireless N Router	192.168.1.1	admin	password
Netgear	WNR3500L Wireless-N Router	192.168.1.1 or www.routerlogin.net	admin	password
Netgear	WPN824 Wireless Router	192.168.1.1	admin	password
TrendNET	TEW-435BRM Wireless Router	192.168.0.1	admin	password
US Robotics (3Com)	Wireless MAXg Router (USR5461)	192.168.2.1	root	admin
ZyXEL	N4100	192.168.1.1	admin	1234

Related Weblinks – Default Router Settings

1. *List of default IP address/password for DSL (high-speed Internet/phone line) modems & routers:*
   http://whirlpool.net.au/wiki/DSL_modemS10_08

2. *List of default router passwords:*
   http://www.cirt.net/passwords

User may either select from already displayed Router manufacturers or enter router manufacturer name into the website **Search** box.

3. *List of network equipment default passwords:*
   http://defaultpassword.com/

User may either select from already displayed Router manufacturers or enter router manufacturer name into the website **Search** box.

4. *Default Password List for Networking Equipment:*
   http://www.beedrop.com/database/Computers/T2LL5282QN/dbindex.html

5. *Default Passwords:*
   http://www.default-password.info/

6. *List of Properties of Networking Equipment:*
   http://www.speedguide.net/broadband-view.php

User must enter router manufacturer **product number** into the website **Search** box.

Last Resort- Reset Router to Factory Default Password

If your Router password appears to have been changed from its factory default and you don't have the password available, **you can as a last resort reset the Router to its factory password default value.** The Router Reset button is usually located at the rear Panel of the Router, as shown in **Figure 5-1**. Follow the below steps:

Figure 5-1. Router Password Reset Button

Verify that the Router power is on.

Press and hold the reset button for 5-10 seconds. It may be necessary to use a paper clip or a pen to press the reset button.

The Router password will then reset to the manufacturer's default value. You can then log into the Router Admin "Internal Website" IP Address and change the Router password to your personally chosen value. Set your Router password to an obscure mixture of letters and numbers **at least 10 characters long** AND IMPOSSIBLE FOR HACKERS TO GUESS.

Appendix B

How to Obtain Router IP Admin Address Using Your PC

In order to perform Router Administration tasks you must identify the Router IP (Internal Admin Website) address.

Below are 2 examples (MS Windows and Apple Mac/ Mac OS X).

In both examples your "Admin" PC must be connected by an Ethernet cable to the Router.

MS Windows 7 Example

From MS Windows "Start" menu type **cmd** into the "Search Programs and Files" text box and press Enter.

Then type **ipconfig** and press Enter.

Your Router's IP is the "Default Gateway," as shown in **Figure B-1.**

Figure B-1. Obtaining "Router IP" Using MS Windows "ipconfig" Command

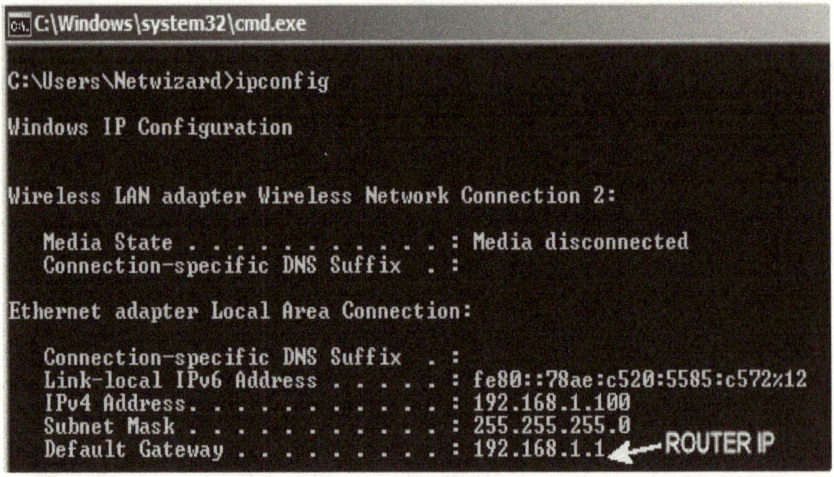

Apple Mac / Mac OS X Example

- For Macintosh PCs: Router IP address is displayed in the TCP/IP Control Panel.

- For Mac OS X PCs: Router IP address is displayed in "System Preferences" in the section "Internet and Network."

Appendix C

Software Vendors

Firewall

1. Check Point Software "Zone Alarm Pro"
(http://www.zonealarm.com/security/en-us/zonealarm-pro-firewall-anti-spyware.htm).

2. GFI/Sunbelt "Software VIPRE Antivirus Premium"
(http://www.vipreantivirus.com/Software/VIPRE-Premium-Antivirus), which incorporates both firewall and antivirus/antispyware functionality.

Antivirus/Antispyware

1. Avast (www.avast.com)
2. Avira "AntiVir" (www.avira.com)
3. "ESET NOD32" Antivirus (www.eset.com)
4. Kaspersky Lab (www.kasperskylab.com)
5. McAfee (http://www.mcafee.com)
6. Microsoft "Security Essentials" Antivirus
7. Symantec (http://us.norton.com/norton/internet-security)
8. Trend Micro (www.trendmicro.com)

Backup and Recovery

1. Norton "Ghost" http://us.norton.com/ghost.

Additional Web Links

10 Tips for Wireless Home Network Security
(http://compnetworking.about.com/od/wirelesssecurity/tp/wifisec
urity.htm)

How do I secure my home WiFi network?
(http://articles.cnn.com/2009-03-
17/tech/pirillo.wireless.security_1_wireless-access-point-
wireless-directory-mac-address?_s=PM:TECH)

Secure Your WiFi (http://www.WiFi.org/secure_your_WiFi)

Wireless Defence (http://www.wirelessdefence.org)

Electronic Frontier Foundation (Privacy Issues)
(www.efff.org/https-everywhere)

Microsoft Malware Protection Center
(http://www.microsoft.com/security/portal/)

Detecting Hostile Websites

For example, the site vwui.com is listed as a malicious site by
both Google and StopBadWare with one listing going back to
2009.

http://safebrowsing.clients.google.com/safebrowsing/diagnostic?
client=Firefox&hl=en-US&site=http://vwui.in/

http://stopbadware.org/reports/90331f78dc600d02b5c6f6e77f80
7915

Recommended Reading

- *Stalking the Stalkers* (Diane Glass, iUniverse, Inc.)

- *Anti-Hacking Toolkit* (Mike Shema et al, McGraw-Hill)

- *Fighting Computer Crime* (Donn B. Parker, Wiley Computer Publishing)

- *Hacker Attack!* (Richard Mansfield, SYBEX Inc)

- *The Unofficial Guide to Ethical Hacking* (Ankit Fadia, Thomson Course Technology)

- *Wireshark & Ethereal –Network Protocol Analyzer Toolkit* (Angela Orebaughet al, Syngress)

- *Wireshark Network Analysis* (Laura Chappell, Founder of Wireshark University ™, Protocol Analysis Institute, LLC)

  .

ABOUT THE AUTHOR

A native of New Jersey, Glenn G. Jacobs holds a B.S. in Electronic Engineering from New Jersey Institute of Technology. His career has involved work as a biomedical electronic engineer, software developer, marketing director, and cyber security engineer and speaker. Jacobs is a member of the Information Systems Security Association (ISSA), the High Technology Crime Investigation Association (HTCIA), Security our eCity, and The Security Network (TSN).

Jacobs was publisher of *The California Eccentric,* a monthly newsletter of political commentary that ran for five years. His first published science fiction short story appeared in *Agony In Black* in 1998. He also co-authored *The Samson Process*, a mystery novel published in 2003.

He is a long-time Grunion Volunteer for the Pepperdine University's Grunion Project. Jacobs has been a member and officer of the San Dieguito-Oceanside Masonic Lodge, and he also is a member of the Knights of Columbus.

He enjoys the beach, hiking, golf, New Age music, reading, and taking nature photos.

www.ingramcontent.com/pod-product-compliance
Lightning Source LLC
Chambersburg PA
CBHW051253050326
40689CB00007B/1177